NAMES & NAMEPLATES
OF
BRITISH STEAM LOCOMOTIVES

1.

LMS
& CONSTITUENTS

D1514164

ALEX HENLEY

HEYDAY PUBLISHING COMPANY

(COVER PHOTOS, DESCENDING SIZE: L. HANSON, A. G. ELLIS
COLLECTION, B. HILTON)

FOR VIC FORSTER

This book is intended as a guide to all the named steam locos owned by the LMS, with minor exceptions. Part A is dedicated to those of LMS design whilst Part B concerns itself with Pre-Grouping locos inherited in 1923. An alphabetical list of locos from both parts is also included at the end of the book for quick and easy reference.

Of all the railway companies grouped into the LMS, thirteen had their own locomotives but only six had named examples. The most notable exceptions were the Midland and Lancashire & Yorkshire Railways. In the main it was the LNWR types which swelled the named ranks with nearly seven hundred locomotives. The Highland Railway contributed a further 87, the Caledonian Railway 5 and the remaining small companies 10. Strictly speaking all the Caledonian locos (including some Highland and other classes) lost their names upon repainting to LMS colours but as this was a gradual process and all ran with names after 1-1-1923 they have been considered named LMS locos. Many locos survived with their original livery until the latter half of that decade such as HR No. 57B 'Lochgorm' (LMS 16119) which was not repainted until 1929.

Abbreviations

B	= Built	RN	= Renamed
c.	= circa	RP	= Repainted
N	= Named	SR	= Streamlining removed
Np	= Nameplate	WD	= Withdrawn
NR	= Name Removed	(1) or (2)	= First (or second)
NX	= Names (& Nos.)		loco with this number
	exchanged with		and/or name in the
PG	= Pre-Grouping		same class
RB	= Rebuilt		

This book has been made possible with the assistance of H. C. Casserley; G. Coltas; B. Ellis; L. Hanson; B. Hilton; J. Hooper; G. M. Kichenside of LGRP; W. Potter; C. Turner of Photomatic and J. F. Ward.

The following publications were consulted in the preparation of this work: A History of Highland Locomotives (Allchin); Engines of the LMS (Rowledge); Locomotives at the Grouping – LMS (Casserley & Johnston); Locomotives of the LNWR (Livesey); Nameplates of the Big Four (Burridge); Register of LNWR Locomotives (Williams).

ISBN 0 947562 01 X

First Published 1984
Copyright Alex Henley 1984

HEYDAY PUBLISHING COMPANY
KINGSWAY HOUSE, 83 CROSBY ROAD NORTH,
CROSBY, MERSEYSIDE, ENGLAND.

PART A

NAMED
LOCOMOTIVES OF LMS DESIGN
(BUILT AFTER 1923)

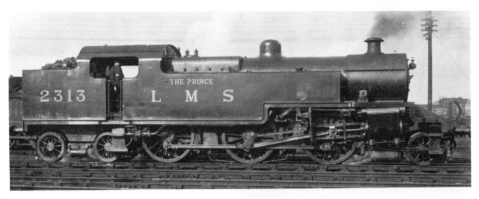

'The Prince' LMS 2313

(Both A. G. Ellis Collection)

LMSR 4P 2-6-4T (1927-1966)

125 Built between 1927-1934 — 1 named
First withdrawals 1959
Last loco in service 1966

LMS No.	BR No.	Name	Notes
2313	42313	The Prince	B 1928 NR 1933

LMSR 'BLACK FIVE' 5P/5F 4-6-0 (1934-1968)

842 Built between 1934-1951 — 4 named
First withdrawal 1961
Last loco in service 1968 — last N loco WD 1968

LMS No.	BR No.	Name	Notes
5154	45154	Lanarkshire Yeomanry	B 1935 N 1937
5156	45156	Ayrshire Yeomanry	B 1935 N 1936
			last N loco
5157	45157	The Glasgow Highlander	B 1935 N 1936
5158	45158	Glasgow Yeomanry	B 1935 N 1936

B. Hilton

4

'The Glasgow Highlander' As BR No 45157   (B. Hilton)

Photomatic

B. Hilton

B. Hilton

5

'Patriot' Class No 5529 between 1937 and 1948 during which time it was nameless. It will be noted that the back-plate which bore it's original name (Sir Herbert Walker K.C.B.) is still in place–See Notes (B. Hilton)

LMSR 'PATRIOT' 5P/6P/7P 4-6-0 (1930-1965)

2 Built in 1930 (incorporating parts & Nos. of ex-LNW 'Claughtons' 5971 & 5902) – 1 named
40 Built between 1932-1933 (as replacements for and incorporating Nos. of ex-LNW 'Claughtons' between 5901 & 6027) – 10 named
10 Built in 1934 – none named
The original 42 members of the class were renumbered in 1934 so as precede those built in 1934
As will be seen below many locos were named in later years (or re-named or both)
First withdrawals 1960
Last loco in service 1965 – named

LMS No.	LMS Renumb.	BR No.	Name(s)	Notes
5971	5500	45500	Patriot	B 1930 N 1937
5902	5501	45501	Sir Frank Ree/St. Dunstans	B 1930 RN 1937
5959	5502	45502	Royal Naval Division	B 1932 N 1937
5985	5503	45503	The Leicestershire Regiment/	B 1932 N 1938
			The Royal Leicestershire Regiment	RN 1948
5987	5504	45504	Royal Signals	B 1932 N 1937
5949	5505	45505	The Royal Army Ordnance Corps	B 1932 N 1947
5974	5506	45506	The Royal Pioneer Corps	B 1932 N 1948
5936	5507	45507	Royal Tank Corps	B 1932 N 1937
6005	5509	45509	Derbyshire Yeomanry	B 1932 N 1951
5942	5511·	45511	Isle of Man	B 1932 N 1938
5966	5512	45512	Bunsen	B 1932 N 1933
5983	5514	45514	Holyhead	B 1932 N 1938
5992	5515	45515	Caernarvon	B 1932 N 1939

No 5500   B. Hilton   No 5501   L. Hanson

No 5507   Photomatic

No 5504   L. Hanson

Above 5511 (L. Hanson) Below 5518 & 5543 (both B. Hilton)

5982	5516	45516	The Bedfordshire and Hertfordshire Regiment	B 1932 N 1938
6006	5518	45518	Bradshaw	B 1933 N 1939
6008	5519	45519	Lady Godiva	B 1933
5954	5520	45520	Llandudno	B 1933 N 1937
5933	5521	45521	Rhyl	B 1933 N 1937
5973	5522	45522	Prestatyn	B 1933 N 1939
6026	5523	45523	Bangor	B 1933 N 1938
5907	5524	45524	Sir Frederick Harrison/Blackpool	B 1933 RN 1936
5916	5525	45525	E. Tootal Broadhurst/Colwyn Bay	B 1933 RN 1937
5963	5526	45526	Morecambe and Heysham	B 1933 N 1937
5944	5527	45527	Southport	B 1933 N 1937
5996	5528	45528	R.E.M.E.	B 1933 N 1960
5926	5529	45529	Sir Herbert Walker K.C.B./Stephenson	B 1933 NR 1937 RN 1948
6022	5530	45530	Sir Frank Ree	B 1933 N 1937 last of class
6027	5531	45531	Sir Frederick Harrison	B 1933 N 1937
6011	5532	45532	Illustrious	B 1933
5905	5533	45533	Lord Rathmore	B 1933
5935	5534	45534	E. Tootal Broadhurst	B 1933 N 1937
5997	5535	45535	Sir Herbert Walker K.C.B.	B 1933 N 1937
6018	5536	45536	Private W. Wood V.C.	B 1933 N 1936
6015	5537	45537	Private E. Sykes V.C.	B 1933
6000	5538	45538	Giggleswick	B 1933 N 1938
5925	5539	45539	E. C. Trench	B 1933
5901	5540	45540	Sir Robert Turnbull	B 1933
5903	5541	45541	Duke of Sutherland	B 1933
—	5543	45543	Home Guard	B 1934 N 1940
—	5545	45545	Planet	B 1934 N 1948
—	5546	45546	Fleetwood	B 1934 N 1938
—	5548	45548	Lytham St. Annes	B 1934 N 1937

Jubilee Class 'Aboukir' as BR No. 45681

(B. Hilton)

LMSR 'JUBILEE' 5P/6P/7P 4-6-0 (1934-1967)

191 Built between 1934-1936 – all named by 1938
First withdrawal 1952 – No. 45637 (Harrow & Wealdstone accident)
Last loco in service 1967

LMS No.	BR No.	Name(s)	Notes
5552	45552	Silver Jubilee	NX 5642 (1935)
5553	45553	Canada	—
5554	45554	Ontario	—
5555	45555	Quebec	—
5556	45556	Nova Scotia	—
5557	45557	New Brunswick	—
5558	45558	Manitoba	—
5559	45559	British Columbia	—
5560	45560	Prince Edward Island	—
5561	45561	Saskatchewan	—
5562	45562	Alberta	last of class
5563	45563	Australia	—
5564	45564	New South Wales	—
5565	45565	Victoria	—
5566	45566	Queensland	—
5567	45567	South Australia	—
5568	45568	Western Australia	—
5569	45569	Tasmania	—
5570	45570	New Zealand	—
5571	45571	South Africa	—
5572	45572	Irish Free State/Eire	RN 1938
5573	45573	Newfoundland	—
5574	45574	India	—
5575	45575	Madras	—
5576	45576	Bombay	—
5577	45577	Bengal	—
5578	45578	United Provinces	—
5579	45579	Punjab	—
5580	45580	Burma	—
5581	45581	Bihar and Orissa	—

Three 'Jubilee' nameplates ex St. Rollox built locos. Note that these had a different style of lettering from the Derby and Crewe engines.
(All B. Hilton)

5582	45582	Central Provinces	—
5583	45583	Assam	—
5584	45584	North West Frontier	—
5585	45585	Hyderabad	—
5586	45586	Mysore	—
5587	45587	Baroda	—
5588	45588	Kashmir	—
5589	45589	Gwalior	—
5590	45590	Travancore	—
5591	45591	Udiapur	—
5592	45592	Indore	—
5593	45593	Kolhapur	loco preserved
5594	45594	Bhopal	—
5595	45595	Southern Rhodesia	—
5596	45596	Bahamas	loco preserved
5597	45597	Barbados	—
5598	45598	Basutoland	—
5599	45599	Bechuanaland	—
5600	45600	Bermuda	—
5601	45601	British Guiana	—
5602	45602	British Honduras	—
5603	45603	Solomon Islands	—
5604	45604	Ceylon	—
5605	45605	Cyprus	—
5606	45605	Falkland Islands	—
5607	45607	Fiji	—
5608	45608	Gibraltar	—
5609	45609	Gilbert and Ellice Islands	—
5610	45610	Gold Coast/Ghana	RN 1958
5611	45611	Hong Kong	—
5612	45612	Jamaica	—
5613	45613	Kenya	—
5614	45614	Leeward Islands	—
5615	45615	Malay States	—

3 Jubilee names ex Nos. 5571, 5732 and 5735. The two lower examples were titles acquired from re-named 'Royal Scots' (See Royal Scot Nos. 6126 & 6129). (All B. Hilton)

5616	45616	Malta/Malta G.C.	RN 1943
5617	45617	Mauritius	—
5618	45618	New Hebrides	—
5619	45619	Nigeria	—
5620	45620	North Borneo	—
5621	45621	Northern Rhodesia	—
5622	45622	Nyasaland	—
5623	45623	Palestine	—
5624	45624	St. Helena	—
5625	45625	Sarawak	—
5626	45626	Seychelles	—
5627	45627	Sierra Leone	—
5628	45628	Somaliland	—
5629	45629	Straits Settlements	—
5630	45630	Swaziland	—
5631	45631	Tanganyika	—
5632	45632	Tonga	—
5633	45633	Trans-Jordan/Aden	RN 1946
5634	45634	Trinidad	—
5635	45635	Tobago	—
5636	45636	Uganda	—
5637	45637	Windward Islands	—
5638	45638	Zanzibar	—
5639	45639	Raleigh	—
5640	45640	Frobisher	—
5641	45641	Sandwich	—
5642	45642	Boscawen	NX 5552 (1935)
5643	45643	Rodney	—
5644	45644	Howe	—
5645	45645	Collingwood	—
5646	45646	Napier	—
5647	45647	Sturdee	—
5648	45648	Wemyss	—
5649	45649	Hawkins	—
5650	45650	Blake	—
5651	45651	Shovell	—

5652	45652	Hawke	—
5653	45653	Barham	—
5654	45654	Hood	—
5655	45655	Keith	—
5656	45656	Cochrane	—
5657	45657	Tyrwhitt	—
5658	45658	Keyes	—
5659	45659	Drake	—
5660	45660	Rooke	—
5661	45661	Vernon	—
5662	45662	Kempenfelt	—
5663	45663	Jervis	—
5664	45664	Nelson	—
5665	45665	Lord Rutherford of Nelson	—
5666	45666	Cornwallis	—
5667	45667	Jellicoe	—
5668	45668	Madden	—
5669	45669	Fisher	—
5670	45670	Howard of Effingham	—
5671	45671	Prince Rupert	—
5672	45672	Anson	—
5673	45673	Keppel	—
5674	45674	Duncan	—
5675	45675	Hardy	—
5676	45676	Codrington	—
5677	45677	Beatty	—
5678	45678	De Robeck	—
5679	45679	Armada	—
5680	45680	Camperdown	—
5681	45681	Aboukir	—
5682	45682	Trafalgar	—
5683	45683	Hogue	—
5684	45684	Jutland	—
5685	45685	Barfleur	—
5686	45686	St. Vincent	—
5687	45687	Neptune	—
5688	45688	Polyphemus	—
5689	45689	Ajax	Np ex LMS 6139
5690	45690	Leander	loco preserved
5691	45691	Orion	—
5692	45692	Cyclops	—
5693	45693	Agamemnon	—
5694	45694	Bellerophon	—
5695	45695	Minotaur	—
5696	45696	Arethusa	—
5697	45697	Achilles	—
5698	45698	Mars	—
5699	45699	Galatea	loco preserved
5700	45700	Britannia/Amethyst	RN 1951
5701	45701	Conqueror	—
5702	45702	Colossus	—
5703	45703	Thunderer	—
5704	45704	Leviathan	—
5705	45705	Seahorse	—
5706	45706	Express	—
5707	45707	Valiant	—
5708	45708	Resolution	—
5709	45709	Implacable	—
5710	45710	Irresistible	—
5711	45711	Courageous	—
5712	45712	Victory	—

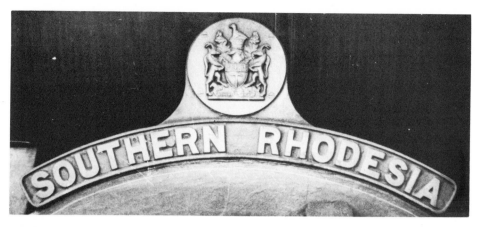

Above & left Two of the three Jubilee names which received badges. The third was 'Ulster'.

All Photographs
Courtesy of B. Hilton

5713	45713	Renown	—
5714	45714	Revenge	—
5715	45715	Invincible	—
5716	45716	Swiftsure	—
5717	45717	Dauntless	—
5718	45718	Dreadnought	—
5719	45719	Glorious	—
5720	45720	Indomitable	—
5721	45721	Impregnable	—
5722	45722	Defence	—
5723	45723	Fearless	—
5724	45724	Warspite	—
5725	45725	Repulse	—
5726	45726	Vindictive	—
5727	45727	Inflexible	—
5728	45728	Defiance	—
5729	45729	Furious	—
5730	45730	Ocean	—
5731	45731	Perseverance	—
5732	45732	Sanspareil	Np ex LMS 6126
5733	45733	Novelty	Np ex LMS 6127
5734	45734	Meteor	Np ex LMS 6128
5735	45735	Comet	Np ex LMS 6129
5736	45736	Phoenix	Np ex LMS 6132
5737	45737	Atlas	Np ex LMS 6134
5738	45738	Samson	Np ex LMS 6135
5739	45739	Ulster	—
5740	45740	Munster	—
5741	45741	Leinster	—
5742	45742	Connaught	—

All photographs courtesy of B. Hilton

Above Royal Scot No. 6164 'The Artists Rifleman'

(W. Potter)

Below The final form of the nameplate of No. 6100 'Royal Scot' in LMS days. The larger of the two arcs was added in 1933 to commemorate the engines tour of North America. It should be noted that the actual loco that travelled was No. 6152 having exchanged numbers and names with 6100

(H. C. Casserley)

LMSR 'ROYAL SCOT' 6P/7P 4-6-0 (1927-1965)

70 Built between 1927-1930 – all named by 1932
1 Built in 1935 (6170) –ex 6399 'Fury' (high pressure loco)
First withdrawals 1962
Last loco in service 1965

LMS No.	BR No.	Name(s)	Notes
6100	46100	Royal Scot	NX 6152 (1933) loco preserved
6101	46101	Royal Scots Grey	—
6102	46102	Black Watch	—
6103	46103	Royal Scots Fusilier	—

15

Royal Scot No. 6137, as was ('Vesta', top) and as re-named (beneath) in 1936. There were 24 other original names that were dispensed with between 1929-36 in favour of regimental titles (see notes of Nos. 6125 to 6145 and note the views opposite). The original names perpetuated those of early locomotives and brass badges placed underneath depicted likenesses of the old designs.

(H. C. Casserley & L. Hanson)

6104	46104	Scottish Borderer	—
6105	46105	Cameron Highlander	—
6106	46106	Gordon Highlander	—
6107	46107	Argyll and Sutherland Highlander	—
6108	46108	Seaforth Highlander	—
6109	46109	Royal Engineer	—
6110	46110	Grenadier Guardsman	—
6111	46111	Royal Fusilier	—
6112	46112	Sherwood Forester	—
6113	46113	Cameronian	—
6114	46114	Coldstream Guardsman	—
6115	46115	Scots Guardsman	last of class loco preserved
6116	46116	Irish Guardsman	—

Above Royal Scot No. 6145 'Condor'   (H. C. Casserley)

Below Royal Scot No. 6130 whilst still named 'Liverpool' together with a close-up of it's plate beneath.
(B. Hilton & J. Ward Collection)

6117	46117	Welsh Guardsman	—
6118	46118	Royal Welch Fusilier	—
6119	46119	Lancashire Fusilier	—
6120	46120	Royal Inniskilling Fusilier	—
6121	46121	H.L.I./Highland Light Infantry, The City of Glasgow Regiment	RN 1949
6122	46122	Royal Ulster Rifleman	—
6123	46123	Royal Irish Fusilier	—
6124	46124	London Scottish	—
6125	46125	Lancashire Witch/3rd Carabinier	RN 1936
6126	46126	Sanspareil/Royal Army Service Corps	RN 1935
6127	46127	Novelty/The Old Contemptible/Old Contemptibles 1914 Aug. 5 to Nov. 22	RN 1936
6128	46128	Meteor/The Lovat Scouts	RN 1936
6129	46129	Comet/The Scottish Horse	RN 1935
6130	46130	Liverpool/The West Yorkshire Regiment	RN 1935
6131	46131	Planet/The Royal Warwickshire Regiment	RN 1936
6132	46132	Phoenix/The King's Regiment Liverpool	RN 1936
6133	46133	Vulcan/The Green Howards	RN 1936
6134	46134	Atlas/The Cheshire Regiment	RN 1936
6135	46135	Samson/The East Lancashire Regiment	RN 1936
6136	46136	Goliath/The Border Regiment	RN 1936
6137	46137	Vesta/The Prince of Wales's Volunteers South Lancashire	RN 1936
6138	46138	Fury/The London Irish Rifleman	RN 1929
6139	46139	Ajax/The Welch Regiment	RN 1936
6140	46140	Hector/The Kings Royal Rifle Corps	RN 1936
6141	46141	Caledonian/The North Staffordshire Regiment	RN 1936
6142	46142	Lion/The York & Lancaster Regiment	RN 1936

'Royal Scot' No. 6121 was given the above title in 1949 (As BR No. 46121). It's LMS name was "H.L.I." (Photomatic)

Top to bottom Nos. 6126, 6136 & 6141

(All L. Hanson)

6143	46143	Mail/The South Staffordshire Regiment	RN 1934
6144	46144	Ostrich/Honourable Artillery Company	RN 1932
6145	46145	Condor/The Duke of Wellington's Regt. (West Riding)	RN 1935
6146	46146	Jenny Lind/The Rifle Brigade	RN 1936
6147	46147	Courier/The Northamptonshire Regiment	RN 1935
6148	46148	Velocipede/The Manchester Regiment	RN 1935
6149	46149	Lady of The Lake/The Middlesex Regiment	RN 1936
6150	46150	The Life Guardsman	—
6151	46151	The Royal Horse Guardsman	—
6152	46152	The King's Dragoon Guardsman	NX 6100 (1933)
6153	46153	The Royal Dragoon	—
6154	46154	The Hussar	—
6155	46155	The Lancer	—
6156	46156	The South Wales Borderer	—
6157	46157	The Royal Artilleryman	—
6158	46158	The Loyal Regiment	—
6159	46159	The Royal Air Force	—
6160	46160	Queen Victoria's Rifleman	—
6161	46161	The King's Own/King's Own	RN 1931
6162	46162	Queen's Westminster Rifleman	—
6163	46163	Civil Service Rifleman	—
6164	46164	The Artists' Rifleman	—
6165	46165	The Ranger 12th London Regt.	—
6166	46166	London Rifle Brigade	—
6167	46167	The Hertfordshire Regiment	—
6168	46168	The Girl Guide	—
6169	46169	The Boy Scout	—
6170	46170	British Legion	B 1935 ex 6399

Royal Scot '3rd Carabinier' as BR No. 46125. This was the final form of the Class. (B. Hilton)

H. C. Casserley

Photomatic

Photos by B. Hilton
unless otherwise
stated

A. G. Ellis Collection

No. 6207 'Princess Arthur of Connaught'   (A. G. Ellis Collection)

LMSR 'Princess Royal' 7P/8P 4-6-2 (1933-1962)

13 Built between 1933-1935 – 12 named
The un-named loco (6202) was turbine powered until rebuilding in 1952 when it was also named – see below
First withdrawal 1954
Last loco in service 1962

LMS No.	BR No.	Name	Notes
6200	46200	The Princess Royal	last of class
6201	46201	Princess Elizabeth	loco preserved
6202	46202	Princess Anne	N 1952 WD 1954
6203	46203	Princess Margaret Rose	loco preserved
6204	46204	Princess Louise	—
6205	46205	Princess Victoria	—
6206	46206	Princess Marie Louise	—
6207	46207	Princess Arthur of Connaught	—
6208	46208	Princess Helena Victoria	—
6209	46209	Princess Beatrice	—
6210	46210	Lady Patricia	—
6211	46211	Queen Maud	—
6212	46212	Duchess of Kent	—

B. Hilton   H. C. Casserley

Above The nameplate from the ill-fated ex-turbomotive, No. 6202, which was deemed beyond repair after the terrible Harrow & Wealdstone accident. Note that it was the only one of the Class to have a support owing to the absence of a wheel splasher. The name was positioned over the forward driving wheels.

(B. Hilton Collection)

Princess Coronation Class locos in both guises: (Upper) No. 6241 'City of Edinburgh' as built with streamlined casing–J. Ward Collection. (Lower) No. 6234 'Duchess of Abercorn', one of the fourteen locos built without dynamics.

A. G. Ellis Collection

LMSR 'Princess Coronation' 7P/8P 4-6-2 (1937-1964)

38 Built between 1937-1948 – all named
24 Built with streamlined casing – see (*) below
First withdrawals 1962
Last loco in service 1964

LMS No.	BR No.	Name	Notes
6220*	46220	Coronation (with Crown above)	B 1937 SR 1946
6221*	46221	Queen Elizabeth	B 1937 SR 1946
6222*	46222	Queen Mary	B 1937 SR 1946
6223*	46223	Princess Alice	B 1937 SR 1946
6224*	46224	Princess Alexandra	B 1937 SR 1946
6225*	46225	Duchess of Gloucester	B 1938 SR 1947
6226*	46226	Duchess of Norfolk	B 1938 SR 1948
6227*	46227	Duchess of Devonshire	B 1938 SR 1946
6228*	46228	Duchess of Rutland	B 1938 SR 1947

Upper & lower B. Hilton Collection. *Centre views* L. Hanson

6229*	46229	Duchess of Hamilton	B 1938 SR 1948
			loco preserved
6230	46230	Duchess of Buccleuch	B 1938
6231	46231	Duchess of Atholl	B 1938
6232	46232	Duchess of Montrose	B 1938
6233	46233	Duchess of Sutherland	B 1938
			loco preserved
6234	46234	Duchess of Abercorn	B 1938
6235*	46235	City of Birmingham	B 1939 SR 1946
			loco preserved
6236*	46236	City of Bradford	B 1939 SR 1947
6237*	46237	City of Bristol	B 1939 SR 1947
6238*	46238	City of Carlisle	B 1939 SR 1947
6239*	46239	City of Chester	B 1939 SR 1947
6240*	46240	City of Coventry	B 1940 SR 1947
6241*	46241	City of Edinburgh	B 1940 SR 1947
6242*	46242	City of Glasgow	B 1940 SR 1947
6243*	46243	City of Lancaster	B 1940 SR 1949
6244*	46244	City of Leeds/King George VI	B 1940 SR 1947
			RN 1941
6245*	46245	City of London	B 1943 SR 1947

Above: The final form of the Princess Coronation Class Loco No. 46232 'Duchess of Montrose'. (W. Potter)

Left: Names ex Nos. 6228 & 6248. (Both B. Hilton Collection)

6246*	46246	City of Manchester	B 1943 SR 1946
6247*	46247	City of Liverpool	B 1943 SR 1947
6248*	46248	City of Leeds	B 1943 SR 1946
6249	46249	City of Sheffield	B 1944
6250	46250	City of Lichfield	B 1944
6251	46251	City of Nottingham	B 1944
6252	46252	City of Leicester	B 1944
6253	46253	City of St Albans	B 1946
6254	46254	City of Stoke-on-Trent	B 1946
6255	46255	City of Hereford	B 1946
6256	46256	Sir William A. Stanier, F.R.S.	B 1947 last of class
—	46257	City of Salford	B 1948

LMSR Experimental 6P 4-6-0 (1929-1935)

1 Built in 1929 – named
Unsuccessful High Pressure loco which was rebuilt as a 'Royal Scot' class (6170 British Legion) in 1935
In service until 1962 (as 46170)

LMS

No.	Name	Notes
6399	Fury	RB as 6170 in 1935 BR No. 46170

PART B

NAMED
LOCOMOTIVES ACQUIRED AT
THE GROUPING
(BUILT PRE-1923)

Ex-LNWR 'PRECEDENT' 1P 2-4-0 (1874-1934)

B. Hilton Collectio

166 Built between 1874-1901
80 survivors on 1/1/1923 – all named
Last loco in service 1934

LMS No.	LMS Renumb.	LNWR No.	Name	Notes
5000	—	2190	Princess Beatrice	—
5001	25001	2191	Snowdon	last of class
5002	—	1170	General	—
5003	—	512	Lazonby	—
5004	—	271	Minotaur	—
5005	—	1522	Pitt	—
5006	—	1527	Raleigh	—
5007	—	379	Sedgwick	—
5008	—	941	Blenkinsop	—
5009	—	1517	Princess Helena	—
5010	—	1480	Newton	—
5011	—	696	Director	—
5012	—	1211	John Ramsbottom	—
5013	—	1212	Pioneer	—
5014	—	1488	Murdock	—
5015	—	1685	Gladiator	—
5016	—	1748	Britannia	—
5017	—	1521	Gladstone	—
5018	—	1672	Talavera	—
5019	—	1531	Cromwell	—
5020	—	1674	Delhi	—
5021	—	2006	Princess	—
5022	—	1525	Abercrombie	—
5023	—	1668	Dagmar	—
5024	—	1675	Vimiera	—
5025	—	1518	Countess	—
5026	—	1519	Duchess	—
5027	—	1520	Franklin	—
5028	—	1666	Ariadne	—
5029	—	1684	Speke	—
5030	—	2002	Madge	—
5031	—	790	Hardwicke	loco preserved
5032	—	1213	The Queen	—
5033	—	1678	Airey	—
5034	—	1745	Glowworm	—
5035	—	304	Hector	—
5036	—	1682	Novelty	—
5037	—	381	Patterdale	—
5038	—	787	Clarendon	—

5039	—	1667	Corunna		—
5040	—	919	Nasmyth		—
5041	—	2005	Lynx		—
5042	—	1173	The Auditor		—
5043	—	2192	Caradoc		—
5044	—	871	Prosperine		—
5045	—	265	Thomas Carlyle		—
5046	—	865	Envoy		—
5047	—	253	President Garfield		—
5048	—	364	Henry Pease		—
5049	—	883	Phantom		—
5050	—	860	Merrie Carlisle		—
5051	—	890	Sir Hardman Earle		—
5052	—	749	Mercury		—
5053	—	945	Humphrey Davy		—
5054	—	2183	Antelope		—
5055	—	514	Lawrence		—
5056	—	477	Caractacus		—
5057	—	866	Courier		—
5058	—	2185	Alma		—
5059	—	2193	Salopian		—
5060	—	619	Mabel		—
5061	—	2176	Robert Benson		—
5062	—	506	Sir Alexander Cockburn		—
5063	—	864	Pilot		—
5064	—	1187	Chandos		—
5065	—	478	Commodore		—
5066	—	2194	Cambrian		—
5067	—	2186	Lowther		—
5068	—	1194	Miranda		—
5069	—	2187	Penrith Beacon		—
5070	—	262	Wheatstone		—
5071	—	480	Duchess of Lancaster		—
5072	—	193	Rocket		—
5073	—	2180	Perseverance		—
5074	—	857	Prince Leopold		—
5075	—	862	Balmoral		—
5076	—	2189	Avon		—
5077	—	1105	Hercules		—
5078	—	870	Fairbairn		—
5079	—	861	Amazon		—

W. Potter   W. Potter

Ex-LNWR 'WATERLOO' 1P 2-4-0 (1889-1936)

90 Built between 1889-1896
35 survivors on 1/1/1923 – all named (includes 5 Eng. Dept.)
Last loco in service 1936

LMS No.	LNWR No.	Name(s)	Notes
5080	748	Waterloo	—
5081	1045	Whitworth	—
5082	733	Chimera	—
5083	814	Henrietta	—
5084	642	Bee	—
5085	901	Hero	—
5086	468	Wildfire/Engineer Northampton	RN 1923
5087	604	Narcissus	—
5088	735	Charon	—
5089	934	North Star	—
5090	124	Marquis Douro	—
5091	634	Ellesmere	—
5092	763	Violet	—
5093	764	Shap	—
5094	609	The Earl of Chester/Engineer Walsall	RN 1923
5095	628	Tartarus	—
5096	817	Constance	—
5097	824	Adelaide	—
5098	486	Skiddaw	—
5099	792	Theorem/Engineer	RN 1923
5100	737	Roberts/Engineer Lancaster	RN 1924
5101	793	Martin/Engineer Watford	RN 1923
5102	1168	Cuckoo	—
5103	732	Hecla	—
5104	794	Woodlark	—
5105	2158	Sister Dora	—
5106	773	Centaur	—
5107	424	Sirius	—
5108	1166 (2)	Wyre (2)	N c.1902
5109	2157	Unicorn	—
—	(885)	Engineer – formerly Vampire	RN 1897
—	(1166) (1)	Engineer Bangor – formerly Wyre (1)	RN 1902
—	(209)	Engineer Crewe – formerly Petrel	RN 1914
		/Engineer South Wales	RN 1932
—	(742)	Engineer Liverpool – formerly Spitfire	RN 1921
—	(2156)	Engineer Manchester – formerly Sphinx	RN 1914

Left
'Engineer Liverpool' at Edge Hill
in LMS livery. (W. Potter)

Right
'Sister Dora' (LMS 5105) whilst
still in LNWR colours. (J. Ward
Collection)

Photomatic

Ex-LNWR 'JUBILEE' 2P 4-4-0 (1897-1925)

40 Built between 1897-1900
9 survivors on 1/1/1923 – all named
37 were rebuilt as 'Renown' class between 1908-1924
Last unrebuilt loco in service 1925

LMS No.	LNWR No.	Name	Notes
5110	1903	Iron Duke	RB as 'Renown' class in 1924
5111	1904	Rob Roy	WD 1923
—	1908	Royal George	WD 1923
5112	1911	Centurion	RB as 'Renown' class in 1924
5113	1912	Colossus	RB as 'Renown' class in 1924
5114	1915	Implacable	RB as 'Renown' class in 1923
5115	1923	Agamemnon	last of class
5116	1927	Goliath	RB as 'Renown' class in 1924
5117	1929	Polyphemus	RB as 'Renown' class in 1924

Ex-LNWR 'ALFRED THE GREAT' 2P 4-4-0 (1901-1928)

40 Built between 1901-1903
15 survivors on 1/1/1923 – all named
33 were rebuilt as 'Renown' class between 1913-1924
Last unrebuilt loco in service 1928

LMS No.	LNWR No.	Name	Notes
5118	1944	Victoria and Albert	—
5119	1952	Benbow	RB as 'Renown' in 1923
5120	1953	Formidable	RB as 'Renown' in 1923
5121	1954	Galatea	RB as 'Renown' in 1924
5122	1955	Hannibal	WD 1923
—	1956	Illustrious	WD 1923
5123	1964	Caesar	RB as 'Renown' in 1924
5124	1966	Commonwealth	—
5125	1967	Cressy	RB as 'Renown' in 1923
5126	1969	Dominion	RB as 'Renown' in 1924
5127	1970	Good Hope	RB as 'Renown' in 1924
5128	1974	Howe	last of class
—	1976	Lady Godiva	WD 1923
5129	1977	Mars	RB as 'Renown' in 1924
5130	1979	Nelson	WD 1923

Facing Page
Top: 'Black Prince' A LNWR 'Jubilee' before conversion to 'Renown' class in 1919 (see 'Renown' class). (B. Hilton Collection)

Middle: 'Royal George' of the LNWR 'Jubilee' class. This loco was one of only three of the class which were never converted to 'Renowns'. It just survived the grouping in 1923 but was never allocated a LMS number. (LGRP, courtesy of David & Charles Ltd)

Bottom: 'Alfred The Great' from the LNWR class of the same name. It was rebuilt as a 'Renown' in 1922 (see 'Renown' class). (B. Hilton Collection)

Ex-LNWR 'RENOWN' 2P 4-4-0 (1908-1931)

70 Built between 1908-1924 using ex-'Jubilee' & 'Alfred the Great' classes
56 constructed by 1/1/1923 (31 'Jub' & 25 'A/Gt')
14 (6 'Jub' & 8 'A/Gt') added 1923/4
Last loco in service 1931

LMS No.	LNWR No.	Name	Notes
5110	1903	Iron Duke	RB ex 'Jub' in 1924
5112	1911	Centurion	RB ex 'Jub' in 1924
5113	1912	Colossus	RB ex 'Jub' in 1924
5114	1915	Implacable	RB ex 'Jub' in 1923
5116	1927	Goliath	RB ex 'Jub' in 1924
5117	1929	Polyphemus	RB ex 'Jub' in 1924
5119	1952	Benbow	RB ex 'A/Gt' in 1923
5120	1953	Formidable	RB ex 'A/Gt' in 1923
5121	1954	Galatea	RB ex 'A/Gt' in 1924
5123	1964	Caesar	RB ex 'A/Gt' in 1924
5125	1967	Cressy	RB ex 'A/Gt' in 1923
5126	1969	Dominion	RB ex 'A/Gt' in 1924
5127	1970	Good Hope	RB ex 'A/Gt' in 1924
5129	1977	Mars	RB ex 'A/Gt' in 1924
5131	1918	Renown	RB ex 'Jub' in 1908
5132	1913	Canopus	RB ex 'Jub' in 1910
5133	1935	Collingwood	RB ex 'Jub' in 1910
5134	1921	John of Gaunt	RB ex 'Jub' in 1913
5135	1971	Euryalus	RB ex 'A/Gt' in 1913
5136	1951	Bacchante	RB ex 'A/Gt' in 1913
5137	1905	Black Diamond	RB ex 'Jub' in 1914
5138	1946	Diadem	RB ex 'A/Gt' in 1914
5139	1945	Magnificent	RB ex 'A/Gt' in 1915
5140	1961	Albermarle	RB ex 'A/Gt' in 1915
5141	1948	Camperdown	RB ex 'A/Gt' in 1915
5142	1930	Ramillies	RB ex 'Jub' in 1916
5143	1959	Revenge	RB ex 'A/Gt' in 1916
5144	1257	Invincible	RB ex 'Jub' in 1916
5145	1943	Queen Alexandra	RB ex 'A/Gt' in 1916
5146	1922	Intrepid	RB ex 'Jub' in 1916
5147	1925	Warrior	RB ex 'Jub' in 1917
5148	1957	Orion	RB ex 'A/Gt' in 1917
5149	1906	Robin Hood	RB ex 'Jub' in 1917
5150	1936	Royal Sovereign	RB ex 'Jub' in 1917
5151	1965	Charles H. Mason	RB ex 'A/Gt' in 1917
5152	1949	King Arthur	RB ex 'A/Gt' in 1918
5153	1960	Francis Stevenson	RB ex 'A/Gt' in 1918
5154	1937	Superb	RB ex 'Jub' in 1919
5155	1916	Irresistible	RB ex 'Jub' in 1919
5156	1901	Jubilee	RB ex 'Jub' in 1919
5157	1902	Black Prince	RB ex 'Jub' in 1919
5158	1939	Temeraire	RB ex 'Jub' in 1919
5159	1909	Crusader	RB ex 'Jub' in 1919
5160	1919	Resolution	RB ex 'Jub' in 1919
5161	1938	Sultan	RB ex 'Jub' in 1920
5162	1932	Anson	RB ex 'Jub' in 1920
5163	1963	Boadicea	RB ex 'A/Gt' in 1920
5164	1968	Cumberland	RB ex 'A/Gt' in 1920
5165	1934	Blenheim	RB ex 'Jub' in 1920
5166	1920	Flying Fox	RB ex 'Jub' in 1920
5167	1975	Jupiter	RB ex 'A/Gt' in 1921
5168	1972	Hindostan	RB ex 'A/Gt' in 1921
5169	1933	Barfleur	RB ex 'Jub' in 1921

5170	1940	Trafalgar	RB ex 'Jub' in 1921
5171	1971	Aurora	RB ex 'A/Gt' in 1921
5172	1910	Cavalier	RB ex 'Jub' in 1921
5173	1928	Glatton	RB ex 'Jub' in 1921
5174	1947	Zillah	RB ex 'A/Gt' in 1921
5175	1973	Hood	RB ex 'A/Gt' in 1921
5176	1931	Agincourt	RB ex 'Jub' in 1921
5177	1978	Merlin	RB ex 'A/Gt' in 1921
5178	1907	Black Watch	RB ex 'Jub' in 1922
5179	1941	Alfred the Great	RB ex 'A/Gt' in 1922
5180	1926	La France	RB ex 'Jub' in 1922
5181	1958	Royal Oak	RB ex 'A/Gt' in 1922
5182	1980	Neptune	RB ex 'A/Gt' in 1922
5183	1924	Powerful	RB ex 'Jub' in 1922
5184	1917	Inflexible	RB ex 'Jub' in 1922
5185	1942	King Edward VII	RB ex 'A/Gt' in 1922
5186	1950	Victorious	RB ex 'A/Gt' in 1922

Top: 'King Arthur' as rebuilt to 'Renown' classification and in LNWR livery (ex 'Alfred the Great' class). (B. Hilton Collection)

Bottom: 'Barfleur' as a 'Renown' class also in LNWR colours (ex 'Jubilee' class). (LGRP, courtesy of David & Charles Ltd)

Ex-LNWR 'PRECURSOR' 2P/3P 4-4-0 (1904-1949)

130 Built between 1904-1907
130 survivors on 1/1/1923 – all named
Last loco in service 1949

LMS No.	LMS Renumb.	LNWR No.	Name	Notes
5187	25187	2023	Helvellyn	—
5188	25188	412	Marquis	—
5189	—	510	Albatross	—
5190	—	639	Ajax	—
5191	—	648	Archimedes	—
5192	—	685	Cossack	—
5193	—	1102	Thunderbolt	—
5194	—	1117	Vandal	—
5195	—	622	Euphrates	—
5196	—	628	Huskisson	—
5197	—	645	Mammoth	—
5198	—	40	Niagara	—
5199	—	1104	Cedric	—
5200	—	1111	Cerberus	—
5201	—	1431	Egeria	—
5202	—	520	Panopea	—
5203	—	2031	Waverley	—
5204	—	184	Havelock	—
5205	—	1115	Apollo	—
5206	—	1545	Cyclops	—
5207	25207	2061	Eglinton	—
5208	—	619	Messenger	—
5209	—	2120	Trentham	—
5210	—	1430	Victor	—
5211	25211	113	Aurania	—
5212	25212	315	Harrowby	—
5213	—	311	Emperor	—
5214	—	1509	America	—
5215	—	2257	Vulture	—
5216	25216	911	Herald	—
5217	—	1114	Knowsley	—
5218	25218	1116	Pandora	—
5219	—	1510	Psyche	—
5220	—	1784	Python	—
5221	—	2202	Vizier	—
5222	—	117	Alaska	—
5223	25223	127	Snake	—
5224	—	229	Stork	—
5225	25225	1301	Candidate	—
5226	—	1396	Harpy	—
5227	—	2007	Oregon	—
5228	—	2012	Penguin	—
5229	—	2115	Servia	—
5230	—	2576	Arab	—
5231	—	2579	Ganymede	—
5232	—	2580	Problem	—
5233	—	2581	Peel	—
5234	—	2582	Rowland Hill	—
5235	—	2583	Moonstone	Last 2P. WD 1935
5236	—	2585	Watt	—
5237	—	234	Pearl	—
5238	—	526	Ilion	—
5239	—	723	Coptic	—
5240	—	837	Friar	—

Above: 'Greyhound' of the 'Precursor' class as LMS 5304 in 1934. (A. G. Ellis Collection)

Below: Three 'Precursor' plates (top to bottom: LMS Nos. 5319, 5188 & 5291). (All courtesy of L. Hanson)

5241	—	1311	Napoleon	—
5242	—	1312	Ionic	—
5243	—	1642	Lapwing	—
5244	—	2017	Tubal	—
5245	25245	561	Antaeus	—
5246	—	675	Adjutant	—
5247	—	772	Admiral	—
5248	—	804	Amphion	—
5249	—	988	Bellerophon	—
5250	—	1433	Faerie Queene	—
5251	—	1650	Richard Trevithick	—
5252	—	1787	Hyperion	—
5253	—	1	Clive	—
5254	—	218	Daphne	—
5255	—	419	Monarch	—
5256	—	665	Mersey	—
5257	—	1011	Locke	—
5258	—	1364	Clyde	—
5259	—	2053	Edith	—
5260	—	2181	Eleanor	—
5261	—	276	Doric	—
5262	—	754	Celtic	—
5263	—	807	Oceanic	—
5264	—	976	Pacific	—
5265	—	1297	Phalaris	—
5266	—	1516	Alecto	—
5270	—	469	Marmion	—
5271	—	812	Gaelic	—
5272	25272	1363	Brindley	—
5273	—	2064	Jason	—
5274	—	638	Hecate	—
5275	—	1439	Tiger	—
5276	—	7	Titan	—
5277	25277	2164	Oberon	—
5278	—	513	Precursor	—
5279	25279	2062	Sunbeam	—
5280	—	2166	Shooting Star	—
5281	—	564	Erebus	—
5282	25282	515	Champion	—
5283	—	2011	Brougham	—
5284	—	333	Ambassador	—
5285	—	1419	Tamerlane	—
5286	25286	1573	Dunrobin	—
5287	25287	365	Alchymist	—
5288	25288	1469	Tantalus	—
5289	—	301	Leviathan	—
5290	—	310	Achilles	—
5291	25291	1395	Harbinger	—
5292	25292	366	Medusa	—
5293	25293	2513	Levens	—
5294	25294	106	Druid	—
5295	—	1723	Scorpion	—
5296	—	659	Dreadnought	—
5297	25297	643	Sirocco	last of class BR No. 58010
5298	25298	60	Dragon	—
5299	25299	1137	Vesuvius	—
5300	25300	1617	Hydra	—
5301	—	300	Emerald	—
5302	25302	1309	Shamrock	—
5303	—	323	Argus	—

5304	25304	302	Greyhound	—
5305	—	303	Himalaya	—
5306	—	1387	Lang Meg	—
5307	25307	305	Senator	—
5308	—	2	Simoom	—
5309	—	2578	Fame	—
5310	25310	1120	Thunderer	—
5311	25311	811	Express	NR 1933
5312	—	2584	Velocipede	NR 1933
5313	—	2577	Etna	—
5314	—	282	Alaric	—
5315	—	2015	Delamere	—
5316	—	1737	Viscount	—
5317	—	374	Empress	—
5318	—	806	Swiftsure	—
5319	25319	990	Bucephalus	—

Above: 'Titan' of the 'Precursor' class whilst still bearing LNWR numbers. It was numbered 5276 by the LMS. (B. Hilton Collection)

Below: Nameplates ex-'Medusa' & 'Greyhound' (LMSR Nos. 5292 & 5304 respectively). (H. C. Casserley & L. Hanson)

Ex-LNWR 'GEORGE THE FIFTH' 2P 4-4-0 (1910-1948)

90 Built between 1910-1915
90 survivors on 1/1/1923 – all named
Last loco in service 1948

LMS No.	LMS Renumb.	LNWR No.	Name	Notes
5320	—	2663	George the Fifth	—
5321	25321	1059	Lord Loch	WD 1948
5322	25322	1294	F. S. P. Wolferstan	—
5323	25323	1583	Henry Ward	—
5324	25324	1725	John Bateson	—
5325	25325	2025	Sir Thomas Brooke	—
5326	25326	2155	W. C. Brocklehurst	—
5327	—	228	E. Nettlefold	—
5328	—	445	P. H. Chambres	—
5329	—	2664	Queen Mary	—
5330	—	1550	Westminster	—
5331	25331	2271	J. P. Bickersteth	—
5332	—	896	George Whale	—
5333	—	1559	Drake	—
5334	25334	2151	Newcomen	—
5335	—	2507	Miles MacInnes	—
5336	—	238	F. W. Webb	—
5337	—	1195	T. J. Hare	—
5338	—	2512	Thomas Houghton	—
5339	25339	2163	Henry Maudslay	—
5340	—	956	Bulldog	—
5341	—	1489	Wolfhound	—
5342	—	1504	Boarhound	—
5343	—	1513	Otterhound	—
5344	25344	1532	Bloodhound	—
5345	25345	1628	Foxhound	—
5346	—	1662	Deerhound	—
5347	25347	1706	Elkhound	—
5348	25348	5000	Coronation	5000th Crewe loco. WD 1940
5349	—	502	British Empire	—
5350	25350	868	India	last of class NR pre 1943
5351	—	882	Canada	—
5352	—	1218	Australia	—
5353	—	1792	Staghound	—
5354	—	2081	New Zealand	—
5355	—	2212	South Africa	—
5356	25356	2291	Gibraltar	—
5357	25357	2495	Bassethound	—
5358	—	2177	Malta	—
5359	—	2498	Cyprus	—
5360	25360	361	Beagle	—
5361	—	888	Challenger	—
5362	25362	1360	Fire Queen	—
5363	—	1394	Harrier	—
5364	—	1623	Nubian	—
5365	25365	1631	Racehorse	—
5366	—	1644	Roebuck	—
5367	—	2089	Traveller	—
5368	—	2494	Perseus	—
5369	25369	1371	Quail	—
5370	—	1417	Landrail	—
5371	25371	1472	Moorhen	—

5372	25372	1595	Wild Duck	—
5373	25373	1681	Ptarmigan	WD 1948
5374	25374	2220	Vanguard	—
5375	—	1714	Partridge	—

Above: "Colwyn Bay" in early LMS livery.
(LGRP, courtesy of David & Charles Ltd.)

Right & Below: Two views of "Coronation's" nameplates. That on the right shows the loco with it's final LMS number. J. Ward Collection

L. Hanson

Above: George the Fifth class 'Richard Arkwright' in LNWR livery. It became LMS No. 5388. (J. Ward Collection)

Below: 'Dovedale', nameplate of No. 5409. (L. Hanson)

5376	25376	1730	Snipe	—
5377	25377	1733	Grouse	—
5378	25378	1777	Widgeon	—
5379	—	1799	Woodcock	—
5380	25380	82	Charles Dickens	—
5381	—	752	John Hick	—
5382	25382	2124	John Rennie	—
5383	—	89	John Mayall	—
5384	—	132	S. R. Graves	—
5385	—	1138	William Froude	—
5386	—	1193	Edward Tootal	—
5387	25387	2154	William Siemens	—
5388	—	2282	Richard Arkwright	—
5389	25389	404	Eclipse	—
5390	—	681	St. George	—
5391	—	845	Saddleback	—
5392	25392	1188	Penmaenmawr	—
5393	25393	1680	Loyalty	—
5394	—	2086	Phaeton	—
5395	25395	2279	Henry Crosfield	—
5396	—	1481	Typhon	—
5397	—	2197	Planet	NR 1933
5398	—	2242	Meteor	NR 1933
5399	—	2428	Lord Stalbridge	—
5400	—	363	Llandudno	—
5401	—	789	Windermere	—
5402	—	984	Carnarvon	—
5403	—	104	Leamington Spa	—
5404	—	226	Colwyn Bay	—
5405	—	1086	Conway	—
5406	25406	2153	Llandrindod	—
5407	—	2233	Blackpool	—
5408	25408	2106	Holyhead	—
5409	25409	2370	Dovedale	—

Ex-LNWR 'EXPERIMENT' 3P 4-6-0 (1905-1935)

105 Built between 1905-1910
105 survivors on 1/1/1923 – all named
Last loco in service 1935

LMS No.	LMS Renumb.	LNWR No.	Name	Notes
5450	—	66	Experiment	—
5451	—	306	Autocrat	—
5452	—	353	Britannic	—
5453	—	372	Belgic	—
5454	—	507	Sarmatian	—
5455	—	565	City of Carlisle	—
5456	25456	893	City of Chester	—
5457	25457	1074	City of Dublin	—
5458	—	1357	City of Edinburgh	—
5459	—	165	City of Lichfield	—
5460	25460	828	City of Liverpool	—
5461	25461	978	City of London	
5462	25462	1405	City of Manchester	—
5463	—	1575	City of Paris	—
5464	—	1669	City of Glasgow	
5465	—	1986	Clanricarde	—
5466	25466	1987	Glendower	—
5467	—	1988	Hurricane	—
5468	—	1989	Lady of the Lake	—
5469	—	1990	North Western	—
5470	—	1991	Palmerston	—
5471	—	1992	President	—
5472	—	1993	Richard Moon	—
5473	25473	1994	Scottish Chief	—
5474	—	61	Atalanta	—
5475	—	222	Ivanhoe	—
5476	—	291	Leander	—
5477	—	667	Mazeppa	—
5478	—	1304	Prometheus	—
5479	25479	1676	Shakespeare	last of class
5480	—	2709	Princess May	—
5481	—	1995	Tornado	—
5482	—	2027	Queen Empress	—
5483	—	2052	Stephenson	—
5484	—	2269	William Cawkwell	—
5485	—	496	Harlequin	—
5486	—	830	Phosphorus	—
5487	25487	902	Combermere	—
5488	25488	937	Princess Alice	—
5489	—	1014	Henry Bessemer	—
5490	—	2112	Victoria	—
5491	25491	1135	Prince George	—
5492	—	1526	Sanspareil	—
5493	—	2161	Jeannie Deans	—
5494	—	322	Adriatic	—
5495	—	884	Greater Britain	—
5496	—	887	Fortuna	—
5497	25497	1020	Majestic	—
5498	—	1483	Redgauntlet	—
5499	—	1490	Wellington	—
5500	—	1553	Faraday	—
5501	—	1571	Herschel	—
5502	25502	2076	Pheasant	—
5503	—	2116	Greystoke	—

5504	25504	2621	Ethelred	—
5505	—	2622	Eunomia	—
5506	25506	2623	Lord of the Isles	—
5507	—	2624	Saracen	—
5508	25508	2625	Buckland	—
5509	25509	2626	Chillington	—
5510	—	2627	President Lincoln	—
5511	25511	2628	Banshee	—
5512	—	2629	Terrier	—
5513	—	2630	Buffalo	—
5514	25514	1406	George Findlay	—
5515	—	1413	Henry Cort	—
5516	—	1477	Hugh Myddleton	—
5517	—	1498	Thomas Savery	—
5518	—	1566	John Penn	—
5519	—	1603	Princess Alexandra	—
5520	—	1649	Sisyphus	—
5521	—	1661	Wordsworth	—
5522	—	1781	Lightning	—
5523	25523	2022	Marlborough	—
5524	—	2637	Babylon	—
5525	25525	2638	Byzantium	—
5526	25526	2639	Bactria	—
5527	—	2640	Belisarius	—
5528	25528	2641	Bellona	—
5529	—	2642	Berenice	—
5530	—	2643	Bacchus	—
5531	25531	2644	Berengaria	—
5532	25532	2645	Britomart	—
5533	—	2646	Boniface	—
5534	—	1412	Bedfordshire	—
5535	—	1418	Cheshire	—
5536	—	1420	Derbyshire	—
5537	—	1455	Herefordshire	—
5538	—	1611	Hertfordshire	—
5539	25539	1616	Lancashire	—
5540	—	71	Oxfordshire	—
5541	—	275	Shropshire	—
5542	—	677	Staffordshire	—
5543	—	1002	Warwickshire	—
5544	—	1534	Westmorland	—
5545	—	1624	Leicestershire	—
5546	—	1652	Middlesex	—
5547	—	1689	Monmouthshire	—
5548	25548	1703	Northumberland	—
5549	—	1471	Worcestershire	—

5550	—	1561	Yorkshire	—
5551	25551	1618	Carnarvonshire	—
5552	25552	1621	Denbighshire	—
5553	—	1658	Flintshire	—
5554	—	1361	Prospero	4-cyl WD 1933

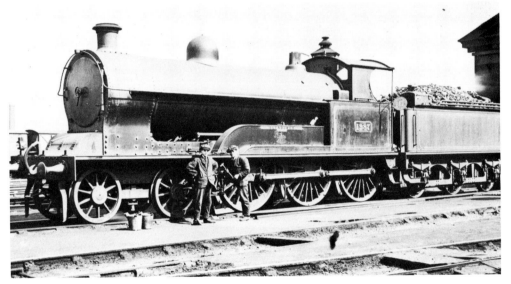

Above: (Top) Experiment class No. 5514 'George Findlay'. (B. Hilton Collection)
(Lower) Experiment 'Glendower' prior to receiving LMS No 5466. (B. Hilton Collection)

Left: Experiment nameplates 'Prospero' (LMS No. 5554) and 'Atalanta' (LMS No. 5474) in preserved guise. (B. Hilton Collection)

Ex-LNWR 'PRINCE OF WALES' 3P 4-6-0 (1911-1949)

245 Built between 1911-1921 – 102 named
1 Built 1924 by LMS – not named (except for 1924 exhibition)
245 survivors on 1/1/1923 – 102 named
Last loco in service 1949 – not named (LMS 25752/BR 58002) WD 5/1949
Last named loco in service 1949 – (Lusitania LMS 25673/BR 58001) WD 1/1949

LMS No.	LMS Renumb.	LNWR No.	Name	Notes
5600	—	819	Prince of Wales	—
5601	25601	1388	Andromeda	—
5602	25602	1452	Bonaventure	—
5603	25603	1454	Coquette	—
5604	25604	1537	Enchantress	—
5605	25605	1691	Pathfinder	—
5606	—	1704	Conqueror	—
5607	25607	1721	Defiance	—
5608	25608	2021	Wolverine	—
5609	—	2359	Hermione	—
5610	—	362	Robert Southey	—
5611	25611	892	Charles Wolfe	—
5612	25612	1081	John Keats	—
5613	25613	1089	Sydney Smith	—
5614	25614	1134	Victor Hugo	—
5615	25615	2040	Oliver Goldsmith	—
5616	25616	2075	Robert Burns	—
5617	25617	321	Henry W. Longfellow	—
5618	25618	479	Thomas B. Macaulay	—
5619	25619	951	Bulwer Lytton	—
5620	25620	2198	John Ruskin	—
5621	25621	2205	Thomas Moore	—
5622	—	2213	Charles Kingsley	—
5623	25623	1679	Lord Byron	—
5624	25624	2249	Thomas Campbell	—
5625	25625	2283	Robert L. Stevenson	—
5626	25626	86	Mark Twain	—
5627	25627	146	Lewis Carroll	—
5628	25628	307	R. B. Sheridan	—
5629	25629	637	Thomas Gray	—
5630	25630	979	W. M. Thackeray	—
5631	25631	1400	Felicia Hermans	—
5632	—	964	Bret Harte	—
5633	25633	985	Sir W. S. Gilbert	—
5634	25634	1321	William Cowper	—
5635	25635	2152	Charles Lamb	—
5636	25636	2293	Percy Bysshe Shelley	—
5637	25637	2377	Edward Gibbon	—
5638	25638	2443	Charles James Lever	—
5639	—	2520	G. P. Neele	—
5640	25640	27	General Joffre	—
5641	25641	88	Czar of Russia	—
5642	25642	122	King of the Belgians	—
5643	25643	160	King of Serbia	—
5644	25644	185	King of Italy	—
5645	25645	877	Raymond Poincare	—
5646	25646	1333	Sir John French	—
5647	25647	2275	Edith Cavell	—
5648	25648	2396	Queen of the Belgians	BR No. 58000
5649	—	2408	Admiral Jellicoe	—
5650	25650	606	Castor	—
5651	25651	745	Pluto	—

5652	—	810	Onyx	—
5653	25653	1352	The Nile	—
5654	25654	1379	Witch	—
5655	25655	1484	Smeaton	—
5656	25656	1084	Shark	—
5657	25657	1346	Trent	—
5658	25658	2417	Atlas	NR 1933
5659	25659	2442	Odin	—
5660	25660	90	Kestrel	—
5661	25661	95	Gallipoli	—
5662	25662	126	Anzac	—
5663	25663	136	Minerva	—
5664	25664	173	Livingstone	—
5665	25665	233	Suvla Bay	—
5666	25666	257	Plynlimmon	—
5667	25667	401	Zamiel	—
5668	25668	446	Pegasus	—
5669	25669	525	Vulcan	—
5670	25670	610	Albion	—
5671	25671	849	Arethusa	—
5672	25672	867	Condor	NR 1933
5673	25673	1100	Lusitania	BR No. 58001 Last N loco
5674	25674	1132	Scott	—
5675	25675	1466	Sphinx	—
5676	25676	1744	Petrel	—
5677	25677	1749	Precedent	—
5678	25678	2055	Milton	—
5679	25679	2063	Hibernia	—
5680	25680	2175	Loadstone	—
5681	25681	2203	Falstaff	—
5682	25682	2339	Samson	NR 1933
5683	25683	1324	Falaba	—

Prince of Wales 'R. B. Sheridan' as LMS No. 5628. (B. Hilton Collection)

5684	25684	2092	Arabic	—
5685	25685	2276	Persia	—
5686	25686	2295	Anglia	—
5687	25687	2300	Hotspur	—
5688	—	2340	Tara	—
5689	25689	2392	Caliban	—
5697	25697	940	Richard Cobden	—
5700	25700	621	Telford	—
5704	25704	1584	Scotia	—
5706	25706	504	Canning	—
5707	25707	974	Hampden	—
5723	25723	522	Stentor	—
5729	25729	1290	Lucknow	—
5736	25736	1325	Disraeli	—
5743	25743	1178	Prince Albert	—
5750	25750	1542	Marathon	—
5753	25753	1694	Premier	—
5754	25754	2516	Dalton	—

Above: Prince of Wales 'Condor' as rebuilt with outside valve gear. Note the raised footplate as compared with the standard design on the previous page. No. 5672 had it's name removed in 1933 to allow LMS Royal Scot No. 6145 to perpetuate the title. (W. Potter)

Below: Two Prince of Wales nameplates, 'Queen of the Belgians' (LMS No. 5648) and 'Shark' (LMS No. 5656). The former loco lasted until Oct. 1948 and was allocated B.R. No. 58000. (Both courtesy of L. Hanson)

Ex-LNWR 'CLAUGHTON' 5P 4-6-0 (1913-1949)

130 Built between 1913-1921 – 60 named
130 survivors on 1/1/1923 – 60 named
Last loco in service 1949 (named up to 1936 – see LMSR 6004)

LMS No.	LNWR No.	Name	Notes
5900	2222	Sir Gilbert Claughton	—
5901*	1161	Sir Robert Turnbull*	—
5902*	1191	Sir Frank Ree*	Parts of this loco used building 'Patriot' No. 5501
5903*	21	Duke of Sutherland*	—
5904	163	Holland Hibbert	—
5905*	650	Lord Rathmore*	—
5906	1159	Ralph Brocklebank	—
5907*	1319	Sir Frederick Harrison*	—
5908	1327	Alfred Fletcher	—
5909	2046	Charles N. Lawrence	—
5910	250	J. A. Bright	—
5911	260	W. E. Dorrington	—
5912	1131	Lord Faber	—
5913	1429	Colonel Lockwood	—
5914	209	J. Bruce Ismay	—
5915	668	Rupert Guinness	—
5916*	856	E. Tootal Broadhurst*	—
5917	1567	Charles J. Cropper	—
5918	2239	Frederick Baynes	—
5919	2401	Lord Kitchener	—
5920	511	George Macpherson	—
5921	695	Sir Arthur Lawley	—
5922	968	Lord Kenyon	—
5923	1093	Sir Guy Calthrop	—
5924	1345	James Bishop	—
5925*	2174	E. C. Trench*	—
5926*	2204	Sir Herbert Walker K.C.B.*	—
5927	2221	Sir Francis Dent	—
5928	2338	Charles H. Dent	—
5929	2395	J. A. F. Aspinall	—
5930	37	G. R. Jebb	—
5931	154	Captain Fryatt	—
5932	155	Sir Thomas Williams	—
5939	2230	Clio	—
5940	1019	Columbus	—
5943	2373	Tennyson	—
5945	2420	Ingestre	—

Claughton 'Vindictive' as LMS No. 5999. (LGRP, courtesy of David & Charles Ltd)

5946	2427	Duke of Connaught	—
5948	2445	Baltic	—
5953	986	Buckingham	—
5964	1914	Patriot	—
5966*	1177	Bunsen	—
5967	1407	L./Corpl. J. A. Christie V.C.	—
5968	1599	John o' Groat	—
5970	2499	Patience	—
5971*	2511	Croxteth	Parts of this loco used building 'Patriot' No. 5500
5975	12	Talisman	—
5976	2035	Private E. Sykes, V.C.	NR 1926 & fixed to loco No. 6015
5979	2268	Frobisher	—
5988	1097	Private W. Wood, V.C.	NR 1926 & fixed to loco No. 6018
5991	2059	C. J. Bowen-Cooke	—
5999	2430	Vindictive	—
6002	30	Thalaba	—
6004	42	Princess Louise	NR 1936 BR No 46004 last of class
6008*	110	Lady Godiva*	—
6011*	150	Illustrious*	—
6015*	158	Private E. Sykes, V.C.*	N 1926 name ex-5976
6017	169	Breadalbane	—
6018*	179	Private W. Wood, V.C.	N 1926 name ex-5988
6019	180	Llewellyn	—
6021	192	Bevere	—
6023	207	Sir Charles Cust	—

*Numbers (& Names) perpetuated amongst the first 42 'Patriots'

Above:
LMS 5927
(W. Potter)

Left:
Nameplate
Ex-5964
(Photomatic)

Ex-LNWR 'SPECIAL TANK' 1F 0-6-0ST (1870-1941)

258 Built between 1870-1880 – none named
(2 Built with square saddle-tanks & named in 1895 – see below)
243 survivors on 1/1/1923 – 2 named
Last loco in service 1941

LMS No.	LNWR No.	Name	Notes
7334	3021	Liverpool	Both locos fitted with condensing apparatus
7335	3186	Euston	and employed from 1895 between Liverpool
			Riverside (MD&HB) and Edge Hill Stations.

Above: Special tank 'Euston' in LNWR colours. It became LMS No. 7335. (B. Hilton Collection)

Below: Nameplate ex-LMS No. 7334. (Photomatic)

Ex-GARSTANG & KNOTT END RY. 0-6-0ST (1897-1926)

2 Built between 1897-1900 – both named
2 survivors on 1/1/1923 (un-numbered previous to this date)
Last loco in service 1926

LMS

No.	Name	Notes
11300	Jubilee Queen	Last of class
11301	New Century	—

Ex-GARSTANG & KNOTT END RY. 0-6-0T (1908-1924)

1 Built in 1908 – named
Survived 1/1/1923 (un-numbered previous to this date)
In service until 1924

LMS

No.	Name	Notes
11302	Knott End	Number never carried

Right: 'New Century' (LMS No. 11301). The name, although not visible here, was painted on the saddle-tank. (B. Hilton Collection)

Below: 'Knott End' which was allocated LMS No. 11302 but never received it. (B. Hilton Collection)

Ex-CLEATOR & WORKINGTON RY. 1F 0-6-0ST (1894-1932)

5 Built between 1894-1920 – all named
5 survivors on 1/1/1923 – all named
Last loco in service 1932

LMS No.	C&W No.	Name	Notes
11564	6	Brigham Hill	—
11565	7	Ponsonby Hall	—
11566	8	Hutton Hall	—
11567	9	Millgrove	—
11568	10	Skiddaw Lodge	last of class

Ex-GARSTANG & KNOTT END RY. 1F 2-6-0T (1909-1927)

1 Built in 1909 – named
Survived 1/1/1923 (un-numbered previous to this date)
In service until 1927

LMS No.	Name	Notes
11680	Blackpool	—

Above: 'Hutton Hall' No. 11566, ex-C&WR No. 8. (J. Ward Collection)

Right: 'Blackpool' of the G&KER which was allocated LMS No. 11680.
(B. Hilton Collection)

Ex-HIGHLAND RAILWAY 'STRATH' 1P 4-4-0 (1892-1930)

12 Built in 1892
6 survivors on 1/1/1923 – all named
Last loco in service 1930

LMS No.	HR No.	Name	Notes
14271	89	Sir George	WD 1930
14272	92A	Strathdearn	WD 1930
14273	94	Strathtay	WD 1925
14274	95	Strathcarron	WD 1930
14275	98	Glentruim	WD 1930
14276	100	Glenbruar	WD 1930

Left: 'Glenbruar' (LMS No. 14276) showing the name over the forward driving wheel. (A. G. Ellis Collection)

Below: 'Glentruim' (LMS No. 14275) at Forres in the year of it's withdrawal, 1930. (H. C. Casserley)

Strath 'Glenbruar' No. 14276 in early LMS livery which employed tender numbering. (H. C. Casserley)

Ex-CALEDONIAN RY. 'DUNALASTAIR II' 2P 4-4-0 (1897-1947)

15 Built in 1897
11 survivors on 1/1/1923 – 1 named
Last loco in service 1947

LMS No.	CR No.	Name	Notes
14335	779	Breadalbane	NR 1925 upon LMS RP

Caledonian Railway No. 779 'Breadalbane'. The name was painted on the splasher of the leading driver. It was renumbered 14335 by the LMS. (A. G. Ellis Collection)

Ex-HIGHLAND RAILWAY 'LOCH' 2P 4-4-0 (1896-1950)

15 Built in 1896, 3 Built in 1917
18 survivors on 1/1/1923 – all named
Last loco in service 1950

LMS No.	HR No.	Name	Notes
14379	119	Loch Insh	BR No. 54379
14380	120	Loch Ness	WD 1941
14381	121	Loch Ericht	WD 1940
14382	122	Loch Moy	WD 1940
14383	123	Loch an Dorb	WD 1934
14384	124	Loch Laggan	WD 1938
14385	125	Loch Tay	BR No. 54385 last of class
14386	126	Loch Tummel	WD 1938
14387	127	Loch Garry	WD 1930
14388	128	Loch Luichart	WD 1930
14389	129	Loch Maree	WD 1931
14390	130	Loch Fannich	WD 1937
14391	131	Loch Shin	WD 1941
14392	132	Loch Naver	WD 1947
14393	133	Loch Laoghal	WD 1934
14394	70	Loch Ashie	WD 1936
14395	71	Loch Garve	WD 1935
14396	72	Loch Ruthven	WD 1934

Left: Compare the styles of lettering applied by the LMS (upper) and the Highland Railways in these two splasher views.
(A. G. Ellis & J. Ward Collections respectively)

Right: (Top to bottom) LMS Nos. 14390, 14396 & 14392. Note that the lower engine has it's name painted in a straight line despite all three views being from the same LMS period. (Top & middle: H. C. Casserley. Bottom: J. Ward Collection)

Ex-HIGHLAND RAILWAY 'SMALL BEN' 2P 4-4-0 (1898-1953)

20 Built between 1898-1906
20 survivors on 1/1/1923 – all named
Last loco in service 1953

LMS No.	HR No.	Name	Notes
14397	1	Ben-y-Gloe	BR No. 54397
14398	2	Ben Alder	BR No. 54398
			last of class
			loco preserved
14399	3	Ben Wyvis	BR No. 54399
14400	4	Ben More	WD 1946
14401	5	Ben Vrackie	BR No. 54401
14402	6	Ben Armin	WD 1939
14403	7	Ben Attow	BR No. 54403
14404	8	Ben Clebrig	BR No. 54404
14405	9	Ben Rinnes	WD 1946
14406	10	Ben Slioch	WD 1947
14407	11	Ben Macdhui	WD 1931
14408	12	Ben Hope	WD 1947
14409	13	Ben Alisky	BR No. 54409
14410	14	Ben Dearg	BR No. 54410
14411	15	Ben Loyal	WD 1936
14412	16	Ben Avon	WD 1947
14413	17	Ben Alligan	WD 1933
14414	38	Ben Udlaman	WD 1933
14415	41	Ben Bhach Ard	BR No. 54415
14416	47	Ben a'Bhuird	BR No. 54416

Above: 'Ben Macdhui' as LMS No. 14407. (H. C. Casserley)

Left: LMS No. 14399. (B. Hilton)

Three 'Small Ben' names with workplates. (All H. C. Casserley)

Ex-HIGHLAND RAILWAY 'LARGE BEN' 2P 4-4-0 (1908-1937)

6 Built between 1908-1909
6 survivors on 1/1/1923 – all named
Last loco in service 1937

LMS No.	HR No.	Name	Notes
14417	61	Ben na Caillich	WD 1936
14418	63	Ben Mheadhouin	WD 1932
14419	64	Ben Mholach	WD 1935
14420	65	Ben a'Chait	WD 1934
14421	60	Ben Bhreac Mhor	WD 1932
14422	62	Ben a'Chaoruinn	last of class

Above, upper: Large Ben LMS No. 14417. (A. G. Ellis Collection)

Above, lower: "Ben a'Chait" as LMS No. 14420 in early livery. (B. Hilton Collection)

Right, upper: "Ben Mholach" No. 14419. (J. Ward Collection)

Right, lower: Ex-GSWR 'Lord Glenarthur' as LMS No. 14509. This engine was the only named GSWR loco to pass into LMSR hands. (B. Hilton Collection)

60

Ex-GLASGOW & SOUTH WESTERN RY. '394' 3P 4-4-0 (1897-1934)

1 Built in 1897
Survived 1/1/1923
In service until 1934

LMS No.	GSW No.	Name	Notes
14509	394	Lord Glenarthur	—

Ex-HIGHLAND RAILWAY 'SNAIGOW' 3P 4-4-0 (1916-1936)

2 Built in 1916
2 survivors on 1/1/1923 – both named
Last loco in service 1936

LMS No.	HR No.	Name	Notes
14522	73	Snaigow	last of class
14523	74	Durn	WD 1935

A. G. Ellis Collection

B. Hilton Collection

Ex-CALEDONIAN RY. '908' 4P 4-6-0 (1906-1935)

10 Built in 1906
10 survivors on 1/1/1923 – 2 named
Last loco in service 1935

LMS No.	CR No.	Name	Notes
14610	909	Sir James King	NR upon LMS RP
14612	911	Barochan	NR upon LMS RP

'Taymouth Castle' as LMS No. 14675. (H. C. Casserley)

Ex-HIGHLAND RAILWAY 'CASTLE' 3P 4-6-0 (1900-1947)

19 Built between 1900-1917
19 survivors on 1/1/1923 – all named
Last loco in service 1947

LMS No.	HR No.	Name	Notes
14675	140	Taymouth Castle	WD 1939
14676	141	Ballindalloch Castle	WD 1937
14677	142	Dunrobin Castle	WD 1939
14678	143	Gordon Castle	WD 1946
14679	144	Blair Castle	WD 1936
14680	145	Murthly Castle	WD 1930
14681	146	Skibo Castle	WD 1946
14682	147	Beaufort Castle	WD 1943
14683	148	Cawdor Castle	WD 1937
14684	149	Duncraig Castle	WD 1940
14685	30	Dunvegan Castle	WD 1945
14686	35	Urquhart Castle	WD 1946
14687	26	Brahan Castle	WD 1935
14688	27	Thurso Castle	WD 1935
14689	28	Cluny Castle	WD 1944
14690	29	Dalcross Castle	last of class
14691	50	Brodie Castle	WD 1938
14692	58	Darnaway Castle	WD 1946
14693	59	Foulis Castle	WD 1935

J. Ward Collection

A. G. Ellis Collection

The Highland lettering (left) was more ornate than the LMS (right). Note also that the lining of the splasher was designed to incorporate curved names in pre-grouping days, not so after 1923.

Top: 'Duncraig Castle' in Highland livery. (J. Ward Collection)

Middle: 'Beaufort Castle' in early LMS livery. (B. Hilton Collection)

Bottom: 'Dunrobin Castle' in later LMS livery. (W. Potter)

64

Ex-CALEDONIAN RY. '49' 4P 4-6-0 (1903-1933)

2 Built in 1903
2 survivors on 1/1/1923 – 1 named
Last loco in service 1933

LMS No.	CR No.	Name	Notes
14751	50	Sir James Thompson	NR upon LMS RP

'Sir James Thompson' in Caledonian livery. (A. G. Ellis Collection)

Ex-CALEDONIAN RY. '903' 4P 4-6-0 (1906-1930)

5 Built in 1906
4 survivors on 1/1/1923 – 1 named
Last loco in service 1930

LMS No.	CR No.	Name	Notes
14752	903	Cardean	NR upon LMS RP

Ex-Caledonian 'Cardean' as LMS No. 14752. (A. G. Ellis Collection)

Above: 'Clan Cameron' as LMS No. 14769 at Inverness in 1930. (H. C. Casserley)

Below: The splasher embellishments of Clans Fraser and Stewart. (Both A. G. Ellis Collection)

Ex-HIGHLAND RAILWAY 'CLAN' 4P 4-6-0 (1919-1950)

8 Built between 1919-1921
8 survivors on 1/1/1923 – all named
Last loco in service 1950

LMS No.	HR No.	Name	Notes
14762	49	Clan Campbell	WD 1947
14763	51	Clan Fraser	WD 1944
14764	52	Clan Munro	BR No. 54764
14765	53	Clan Stewart	WD 1945
14766	54	Clan Chattan	WD 1944
14767	55	Clan Mackinnon	BR No. 54767 last of class
14768	56	Clan Mackenzie	WD 1945
14769	57	Clan Cameron	WD 1943

'Clan Munro' in early LMS livery. (H. C. Casserley)

Ex-HIGHLAND RAILWAY '101' 4-4-0T (1892-1934)

5 Built between 1892-1893
5 survivors on 1/1/1923 – 1 named
Last loco in service 1934

LMS No.	HR No.	Name	Notes
15014	102	Munlochy	NR upon LMS RP

Ex-HR 'Munlochy' as LMS No. 15014 in 1926. The painted name had occupied the tank sides. (A. G. Ellis Collection)

Ex-HIGHLAND RAILWAY '13' 0-4-4T (1890-1929)

1 Built in 1890 (as Saddle-Tank, RB 1901 as side-Tank)
Survived 1/1/1923 – named
In service until 1929

LMS No.	HR No.	Name	Notes
15050	53A	Lybster	NR upon LMS RP

Ex-HR 'Lybster' as LMS No. 15050. As with all HR engines, the name was painted and in this case on the tank sides. (J. Ward Collection)

Below: Ex-HR 'Strathpeffer' as LMS No. 15051. (A. G. Ellis Collection)

Ex-HIGHLAND RAILWAY '25' 0-4-4T (1905-1957)

4 Built between 1905-1906
4 survivors on 1/1/1923 – 2 named
Last loco in service 1957

LMS No.	HR No.	Name	Notes
15051	25	Strathpeffer	NR upon LMS RP
			BR No. 55051
			WD 1956
15052	40	Gordon Lennox	NR upon LMS RP
			WD 1930

Ex-HIGHLAND RAILWAY '56' 0-6-0T (1869-1932)

3 Built between 1869-1874
3 survivors on 1/1/1923 – all named
Last loco in service 1932

LMS No.	HR No.	Name	Notes
16118	56B	Dornoch	NR upon LMS RP WD 1928
16119	57B	Lochgorm	NR upon LMS RP in 1929 (last HR loco with PG livery) WD 1932 last of class
16383	49A	Fort George	NR upon LMS RP WD 1927

Above: Ex-HR 'Lochgorm' as LMS No. 16119. Note the detail differences with the earlier photograph below (bunker etc).
Below: 16119 in it's pre-grouping state. The loco lasted until 1929 in this livery (see above notes). Both photos: J. Ward Collection

69

ALPHABETICAL LISTING OF ALL NAMED LMS LOCOMOTIVES

The numbers alongside each name relate to LMS sequence only. Space does not permit the inclusion of any renumberings. Note that for continuity purposes the 'Patriot' class only are listed with their later LMS numbers. It will be noted that certain names appear more than once and to assist with identification of Pre-Grouping types the following prefixes are explained:

L = LNWR   GKE = Garstang & Knott End Ry.   H = Highland Ry.   CW = Cleator & Workington Ry.   GSW = Glasgow & S. Western Ry.   C = Caledonian Ry.

A

Name	Number
Abercrombie	L5022
Aboukir	5681
Achilles	5697
Achilles	L5290
Adelaide	L5097
Aden	5633
Adjutant	L5246
Admiral	L5247
Admiral Jellicoe	L5649
Adriatic	L5494
Agamemnon	5693
Agamemnon	L5115
Agincourt	L5176
Airey	L5033
Ajax	5689
Ajax	6139
Ajax	L5190
Alaric	L5314
Alaska	L5222
Albatross	L5189
Albemarle	L5140
Alberta	5562
Albion	L5670
Alchymist	L5287
Alecto	L5266
Alfred Fletcher	L5908
Alfred the Great	L5179
Alma	L5058
Amazon	L5079
Ambassador	L5284
America	L5214
Amethyst	5700
Amphion	L5248
Andromeda	L5601
Anglia	L5686
Anson	5672
Anson	L5162
Antaeus	L5245
Antelope	L5054
Anzac	L5662
Apollo	L5205
Arab	L5230
Arabic	L5684
Archimedes	L5191
Arethusa	5696
Arethusa	L5671
Argus	L5303
Argyll and Sutherland Highlander	6107
Ariadne	L5028
Armada	5679
Assam	5583

Name	Number
Atalanta	L5474
Atlas	5737
Atlas	6134
Atlas	L5658
Aurania	L5211
Aurora	L5171
Australia	5563
Australia	L5352
Autocrat	L5451
Avon	L5076
Ayrshire Yeomanry	5156

B

Name	Number
Babylon	L5524
Bacchante	L5136
Bacchus	L5530
Bactria	L5526
Bahamas	5596
Ballindalloch Castle	H14676
Balmoral	L5075
Baltic	L5948
Bangor	5523
Banshee	L5511
Barbados	5597
Barfleur	5685
Barfleur	L5169
Barham	5653
Barochan	C14612
Baroda	5587
Bassethound	L5357
Basutoland	5598
Beagle	L5360
Beatty	5677
Beaufort Castle	H14682
Bechuanaland	5599
Bedfordshire	L5534
Bee	L5084
Belgic	L5453
Belisarius	L5527
Bellerophon	5694
Bellerophon	L5249
Bellona	L5528
Ben A'Bhuird	H14416
Ben A'Chait	H14420
Ben A'Chaoruinn	H14422
Ben Alder	H14398
Ben Alisky	H14409
Ben Alligan	H14413
Ben Armin	H14402
Ben Attow	H14403
Ben Avon	H14412

Ben Bhach Ard	H14415	Bucephalus	L5319
Ben Bhreac Mhor	H14421	Buckingham	L5953
Benbow	L5119	Buckland	L5508
Ben Clebrig	H14404	Buffalo	L5513
Ben Dearg	H14410	Bulldog	L5340
Bengal	5577	Bulwer Lytton	L5619
Ben Hope	H14408	Bunsen	5512
Ben Loyal	H14411	Bunsen	L5966
Ben Macdhui	H14407	Burma	5580
Ben Mheadhouin	H14418	Byzantium	L5525
Ben Mholach	H14419		
Ben More	H14400	**C**	
Ben Na Caillich	H14417	Caernarvon	5515
Ben Rinnes	H14405	Caesar	L5123
Ben Slioch	H14406	Caledonian	6141
Ben Udlaman	H14414	Caliban	L5689
Ben Vrackie	H14401	Cambrian	L5066
Ben Wyvis	H14399	Cameron Highlander	6105
Ben-y-Gloe	H14397	Cameronian	6113
Berengaria	L5531	Camperdown	5680
Berenice	L5529	Camperdown	L5141
Bermuda	5600	Canada	5553
Bevere	L6021	Canada	L5351
Bhopal	5594	Candidate	L5225
Bihar and Orissa	5581	Canning	L5706
Black Diamond	L5137	Canopus	L5132
Blackpool	5524	Captain Fryatt	L5931
Blackpool	GKE11680	Caractacus	L5056
Blackpool	L5407	Caradoc	L5043
Black Prince	L5157	Cardean	C14752
Black Watch	6102	Carnarvon	L5402
Black Watch	L5178	Carnarvonshire	L5551
Blair Castle	H14679	Castor	L5650
Blake	5650	Cavalier	L5172
Blenheim	L5165	Cawdor Castle	H14683
Blenkinsop	L5008	Cedric	L5199
Bloodhound	L5344	Celtic	L5262
Boadicea	L5163	Centaur	L5106
Boarhound	L5342	Central Provinces	5582
Bombay	5576	Centurion	L5112
Bonaventure	L5602	Cerberus	L5200
Boniface	L5533	Ceylon	5604
Boscawen	5642	Challenger	L5361
Bradshaw	5518	Champion	L5282
Brahan Castle	H14687	Chandos	L5064
Breadalbane	C14335	Charles Dickens	L5380
Breadalbane	L6017	Charles H. Dent	L5928
Bret Harte	L5632	Charles H. Mason	L5151
Brigham Hill	CW11564	Charles James Lever	L5638
Brindley	L5272	Charles J. Cropper	L5917
Britannia	5700	Charles Kingsley	L5622
Britannia	L5016	Charles Lamb	L5635
Britannic	L5452	Charles N. Lawrence	L5909
British Columbia	5559	Charles Wolfe	L5611
British Empire	L5349	Charon	L5088
British Guiana	5601	Cheshire	L5535
British Honduras	5602	Chillington	L5509
British Legion	6170	Chimera	L5082
Britomart	L5532	City of Birmingham	6235
Brodie Castle	H14691	City of Bradford	6236
Brougham	L5283	City of Bristol	6237

City of Carlisle	6238	Condor	6145
City of Carlisle	L5455	Condor	L5672
City of Chester	6239	Connaught	5742
City of Chester	L5456	Conqueror	5701
City of Coventry	6240	Conqueror	L5606
City of Dublin	L5457	Constance	L5096
City of Edinburgh	6241	Conway	L5405
City of Edinburgh	L5458	Coptic	L5239
City of Glasgow	6242	Coquette	L5603
City of Glasgow	L5464	Cornwallis	5666
City of Hereford	6255	Coronation	6220
City of Lancaster	6243	Coronation	L5348
City of Leeds	6244	Corunna	L5039
City of Leeds	6248	Cossack	L5192
City of Leicester	6252	Countess	L5025
City of Lichfield	6250	Courageous	5711
City of Lichfield	L5459	Courier	6147
City of Liverpool	6247	Courier	L5057
City of Liverpool	L5460	Cressy	L5125
City of London	6245	Cromwell	L5019
City of London	L5461	Croxteth	L5971
City of Manchester	6246	Crusader	L5159
City of Manchester	L5462	Cuckoo	L5102
City of Nottingham	6251	Cumberland	L5164
City of Paris	L5463	Cyclops	5692
City of St. Albans	6253	Cyclops	L5206
City of Salford	(46257)	Cyprus	5605
City of Sheffield	6249	Cyprus	L5359
City of Stoke-on-Trent	6254	Czar of Russia	L5641
Civil Service Rifleman	6163		
C. J. Bowen-Cooke	L5991	**D**	
Clan Cameron	H14769	Dagmar	L5023
Clan Campbell	H14762	Dalcross Castle	H14690
Clan Chattan	H14766	Dalton	L5754
Clan Fraser	H14763	Daphne	L5254
Clan Mackenzie	H14768	Darnaway Castle	H14692
Clan Mackinnon	H14767	Dauntless	5717
Clan Munro	H14764	Deerhound	L5346
Clanricarde	L5465	Defence	5722
Clan Stewart	H14765	Defiance	5728
Clarendon	L5038	Defiance	L5607
Clio	L5939	Delamere	L5315
Clive	L5253	Delhi	L5020
Cluny Castle	H14689	Denbighshire	L5552
Clyde	L5258	Derbyshire	L5536
Cochrane	5656	Derbyshire Yeomanry	5509
Codrington	5676	De Robeck	5678
Coldstream Guardsman	6114	Diadem	L5138
Collingwood	5645	Director	L5011
Collingwood	L5133	Disraeli	L5736
Colonel Lockwood	L5913	Dominion	L5126
Colossus	5702	Doric	L5261
Colossus	L5113	Dornoch	H16118
Columbus	L5940	Dovedale	L5409
Colwyn Bay	5525	Dragon	L5298
Colwyn Bay	L5404	Drake	5659
Combermere	L5487	Drake	L5333
Comet	5735	Dreadnought	5718
Comet	6129	Dreadnought	L5296
Commodore	L5065	Druid	L5294
Commonwealth	L5124	Duchess	L5026

Duchess of Abercorn	6234	Falstaff	L5681
Duchess of Atholl	6231	Fame	L5309
Duchess of Buccleuch	6230	Faraday	L5500
Duchess of Devonshire	6227	Fearless	5723
Duchess of Gloucester	6225	Felicia Hermans	L5631
Duchess of Hamilton	6229	Fiji	5607
Duchess of Kent	6212	Fire Queen	L5362
Duchess of Lancaster	L5071	Fisher	5669
Duchess of Montrose	6232	Fleetwood	5546
Duchess of Norfolk	6226	Flintshire	L5553
Duchess of Rutland	6228	Flying Fox	L5166
Duchess of Sutherland	6233	Formidable	L5120
Duke of Connaught	L5946	Fort George	H16383
Duke of Sutherland	5541	Fortuna	L5496
Duke of Sutherland	L5903	Foulis Castle	H14693
Duncan	5674	Foxhound	L5345
Duncraig Castle	H14684	Francis Stevenson	L5153
Dunrobin	L5286	Franklin	L5027
Dunrobin Castle	H14677	Frederick Baynes	L5918
Dunvegan Castle	H14685	Friar	L5240
Durn	H14523	Frobisher	5640
		Frobisher	L5979
E		F. S. P. Wolferstan	L5322
Eclipse	L5389	Furious	5729
E. C. Trench	5539	Fury	6138
E. C. Trench	L5925	Fury	6399
Edith	L5259	F. W. Webb	L5336
Edith Cavell	L5647		
Edward Gibbon	L5637	**G**	
Edward Tootal	L5386	Gaelic	L5271
Egeria	L5201	Galatea	5699
Eglinton	L5207	Galatea	L5121
Eire	5572	Gallipoli	L5661
Eleanor	L5260	Ganymede	L5231
Elkhound	L5347	General	L5002
Ellesmere	L5091	General Joffre	L5640
Emerald	L5301	George Findlay	L5514
Emperor	L5213	George Macpherson	L5920
Empress	L5317	George the Fifth	L5320
Enchantress	L5604	George Whale	L5332
E. Nettlefold	L5327	Ghana	5610
Envoy	L5046	Gibraltar	5608
Erebus	L5281	Gibraltar	L5356
Ethelred	L5504	Giggleswick	5538
Etna	L5313	Gilbert and Ellice Islands	5609
E. Tootal Broadhurst	5525	Gladiator	L5015
E. Tootal Broadhurst	5534	Gladstone	L5017
E. Tootal Broadhurst	L5916	Glasgow Yeomanry	5158
Eunomia	L5505	Glatton	L5173
Euphrates	L5195	Glenbruar	H14276
Euryalus	L5135	Glendower	L5466
Euston	L7335	Glentruim	H14275
Experiment	L5450	Glorious	5719
Express	5706	Glowworm	L5034
Express	L5311	Gold Coast	5610
		Goliath	6136
F		Goliath	L5116
Faerie Queen	L5250	Good Hope	L5127
Fairbairn	L5078	Gordon Castle	H14678
Falaba	L5683	Gordon Highlander	6106
Falkland Islands	5606	Gordon Lennox	H15052

G. P. Neele	L5639	Hugh Myddleton	L5516
Greater Britain	L5495	Humphrey Davy	L5053
Grenadier Guardsman	6110	Hurricane	L5467
Greyhound	L5304	Huskisson	L5196
Greystoke	L5503	Hutton Hall	CW11566
G. R. Jebb	L5930	Hyderabad	5585
Grouse	L5377	Hydra	L5300
Gwalior	5589	Hyperion	L5252

H

I

Hampden	L5707	Ilion	L5238
Hannibal	L5122	Illustrious	5532
Harbinger	L5291	Illustrious (Alf./Gt.)	L—
Hardwicke	L5031	Illustrious	L6011
Hardy	5675	Implacable	5709
Harlequin	L5485	Implacable	L5114
Harpy	L5226	Impregnable	5721
Harrier	L5363	India	5574
Harrowby	L5212	India	L5350
Havelock	L5204	Indomitable	5720
Hawke	5652	Indore	5592
Hawkins	5649	Inflexible	5727
Hecate	L5274	Inflexible	L5184
Hecla	L5103	Ingestre	L5945
Hector	6140	Intrepid	L5146
Hector	L5035	Invincible	5715
Helvellyn	L5187	Invincible	L5144
Henrietta	L5083	Ionic	L5242
Henry Bessemer	L5489	Irish Free State	5572
Henry Cort	L5515	Irish Guardsman	6116
Henry Crosfield	L5395	Iron Duke	L5110
Henry Maudslay	L5339	Irresistible	5710
Henry Pease	L5048	Irresistible	L5155
Henry Ward	L5323	Isle of Man	5511
Henry W. Longfellow	L5617	Ivanhoe	L5475
Herald	L5216		

J

Hercules	L5077		
Herefordshire	L5537	J. A. Bright	L5910
Hermione	L5609	J. A. F. Aspinall	L5929
Hero	L5085	Jamaica	5612
Herschel	L5501	James Bishop	L5924
Hertfordshire	L5538	Jason	L5273
Hibernia	L5679	J. Bruce Ismay	L5914
Highland Light Infantry,		Jeannie Deans	L5493
The City of Glasgow Regt.	6121	Jellicoe	5667
Himalaya	L5305	Jenny Lind	6146
Hindostan	L5168	Jervis	5663
H.L.I.	6121	John Bateson	L5324
Hogue	5683	John Hick	L5381
Holland Hibbert	L5904	John Keats	L5612
Holyhead	5514	John Mayall	L5383
Holyhead	L5408	John of Gaunt	L5134
Home Guard	5543	John o' Groat	L5968
Hong Kong	5611	John Penn	L5518
Honourable Artillery Co.	6144	John Ramsbottom	L5012
Hood	5654	John Rennie	L5382
Hood	L5175	John Ruskin	L5620
Hotspur	L5687	J. P. Bickersteth	L5331
Howard of Effingham	5670	Jubilee	L5156
Howe	5644	Jubilee Queen	GKE11300
Howe	L5128	Jupiter	L5167
		Jutland	5684

74

K

Kashmir	5588
Keith	5655
Kempenfelt	5662
Kenya	5613
Keppel	5673
Kestrel	L5660
Keyes	5658
King Arthur	L5152
King Edward VII	L5185
King George VI	6244
King of Italy	L5644
King of Serbia	L5643
King of the Belgians	L5642
King's Own	6161
Knott End	GKE11302
Knowsley	L5217
Kolhapur	5593

L

Lady Godiva	5519
Lady Godiva (Alf./Gt.)	L—
Lady Godiva	L6008
Lady of the Lake	6149
Lady of the Lake	L5468
Lady Patricia	6210
La France	L5180
Lanarkshire Yeomanry	5154
Lancashire	L5539
Lancashire Fusilier	6119
Lancashire Witch	6125
Landrail	L5370
Lang Meg	L5306
Lapwing	L5243
Lawrence	L5055
Lazonby	L5003
L./Corpl. J. A. Christie V.C.	L5967
Leamington Spa	L5403
Leander	5690
Leander	L5476
Leeward Islands	5614
Leicestershire	L5545
Leinster	5741
Levens	L5293
Leviathan	5704
Leviathan	L5289
Lewis Carroll	L5627
Lightning	L5522
Lion	6142
Liverpool	6130
Liverpool	L7334
Livingston	L5664
Llandrindod	L5406
Llandudno	5520
Llandudno	L5400
Llewellyn	L6019
Loadstone	L5680
Loch an Dorb	H14383
Loch Ashie	H14394
Loch Ericht	H14381
Loch Fannich	H14390

Loch Garry	H14387
Loch Garve	H14395
Lochgorm	H16119
Loch Insh	H14379
Loch Laggan	H14384
Loch Laoghal	H14393
Loch Luichart	H14388
Loch Maree	H14389
Loch Moy	H14382
Loch Naver	H14392
Loch Ness	H14380
Loch Ruthven	H14396
Loch Shin	H14391
Loch Tay	H14385
Loch Tummel	H14386
Locke	L5257
London Rifle Brigade	6166
London Scottish	6124
Lord Byron	L5623
Lord Faber	L5912
Lord Glenarthur	GSW14509
Lord Kenyon	L5922
Lord Kitchener	L5919
Lord Loch	L5321
Lord of the Isles	L5506
Lord Rathmore	5533
Lord Rathmore	L5905
Lord Rutherford of Nelson	5665
Lord Stalbridge	L5399
Lowther	L5067
Loyalty	L5393
Lucknow	L5729
Lusitania	L5673
Lybster	H15050
Lynx	L5041
Lytham St. Annes	5548

M

Mabel	L5060
Madden	5668
Madge	L5030
Madras	5575
Magnificent	L5139
Mail	6143
Majestic	L5497
Malay States	5615
Malta	5616
Malta	L5358
Malta G.C.	5616
Mammoth	L5197
Manitoba	5558
Marathon	L5750
Mark Twain	L5626
Marlborough	L5523
Marmion	L5270
Marquis	L5188
Marquis Douro	L5090
Mars	5698
Mars	L5129
Martin	L5101
Mauritius	5617

Mazeppa	L5477	**O**	
Medusa	L5292	Oberon	L5277
Mercury	L5052	Ocean	5730
Merlin	L5177	Oceanic	L5263
Merrie Carlisle	L5050	Odin	L5659
Mersey	L5256	Old Contemptibles 1914	
Messenger	L5208	Aug. 5 to Nov. 22	6127
Meteor	5734	Oliver Goldsmith	L5615
Meteor	6128	Ontario	5554
Meteor	L5398	Onyx	L5652
Middlesex	L5546	Oregon	L5227
Miles MacInnes	L5335	Orion	5691
Milgrove	CW11567	Orion	L5148
Milton	L5678	Ostrich	6144
Minerva	L5663	Otterhound	L5343
Minotaur	5695	Oxfordshire	L5540
Minotaur	L5004		
Miranda	L5068		
Monarch	L5255	**P**	
Monmouthshire	L5547	Pacific	L5264
Moonstone	L5235	Palestine	5623
Moorhen	L5371	Palmerston	L5470
Morecambe and Heysham	5526	Pandora	L5218
Munlochy	H15014	Panopea	L5202
Munster	5740	Partridge	L5375
Murdock	L5014	Pathfinder	L5605
Murthly Castle	H14680	Patience	L5970
Mysore	5586	Patriot	5500
		Patriot	L5964
N		Patterdale	L5037
Napier	5646	Pearl	L5237
Napoleon	L5241	Peel	L5233
Narcissus	L5087	Pegasus	L5668
Nasmyth	L5040	Penguin	L5228
Nelson	5664	Penmaenmawr	L5392
Nelson	L5130	Penrith Beacon	L5069
Neptune	5687	Percy Bysshe Shelley	L5636
Neptune	L5182	Perseus	L5368
New Brunswick	5557	Perseverance	5731
New Century	GKE11301	Perseverance	L5073
Newcomen	L5334	Persia	L5685
Newfoundland	5573	Petrel	L5676
New Hebrides	5618	Phaeton	L5394
New South Wales	5564	Phalaris	L5265
Newton	L5010	Phantom	L5049
New Zealand	5570	P. H. Chambres	L5328
New Zealand	L5354	Pheasant	L5502
Niagara	L5198	Phoenix	5736
Nigeria	5619	Phoenix	6132
North Borneo	5620	Phosphorus	L5486
Northern Rhodesia	5621	Pilot	L5063
North Star	L5089	Pioneer	L5013
Northumberland	L5548	Pitt	L5005
North Western	L5469	Planet	5545
North West Frontier	5584	Planet	6131
Nova Scotia	5556	Planet	L5397
Novelty	5733	Pluto	L5651
Novelty	6127	Plynlimmon	L5666
Novelty	L5036	Polyphemus	5688
Nubian	L5364	Polyphemus	L5117
Nyasaland	5622	Ponsonby Hall	CW11565

Powerful	L5183	**R**	
Precedent	L5677	Racehorse	L5365
Precursor	L5278	Raleigh	5639
Premier	L5753	Raleigh	L5006
President	L5471	Ralph Brocklebank	L5906
President Garfield	L5047	Ramillies	L5142
President Lincoln	L5510	Raymond Poincare	L5645
Prestatyn	5522	R. B. Sheridan	L5628
Prince Albert	L5743	Redgauntlet	L5498
Prince Edward Island	5560	R.E.M.E.	5528
Prince George	L5491	Renown	5713
Prince Leopold	L5074	Renown	L5131
Prince of Wales	L5600	Repulse	5725
Prince Rupert	5671	Resolution	5708
Princess	L5021	Resolution	L5160
Princess Alexandra	6224	Revenge	5714
Princess Alexandra	L5519	Revenge	L5143
Princess Alice	6223	Rhyl	5521
Princess Alice	L5488	Richard Arkwright	L5388
Princess Anne	(46202)	Richard Cobden	L5697
Princess Arthur of Connaught	6207	Richard Moon	L5472
Princess Beatrice	6209	Richard Trevithick	L5251
Princess Beatrice	L5000	Robert Benson	L5061
Princess Elizabeth	6201	Robert Burns	L5616
Princess Helena	L5009	Robert L. Stevenson	L5625
Princess Helena Victoria	6208	Roberts	L5100
Princess Louise	6204	Robert Southey	L5610
Princess Louise	L6004	Robin Hood	L5149
Princess Margaret Rose	6203	Rob Roy	L5111
Princess Marie Louise	6206	Rocket	L5072
Princess May	L5480	Rodney	5643
Princess Victoria	6205	Roebuck	L5366
Private E. Sykes V.C.	5537	Rooke	5660
Private E. Sykes V.C.	L5976	Rowland Hill	L5234
Private E. Sykes V.C.	L6015	Royal Army Service Corps	6126
Private W. Wood V.C.	5536	Royal Engineer	6109
Private W. Wood V.C.	L5988	Royal Fusilier	6111
Private W. Wood V.C.	L6018	Royal George (Jubilee)	L—
Problem	L5232	Royal Inniskilling Fusilier	6120
Prometheus	L5478	Royal Irish Fusilier	6123
Prosperine	L5044	Royal Naval Division	5502
Prospero	L5554	Royal Oak	L5181
Psyche	L5219	Royal Scot	6100
Ptarmigan	L5373	Royal Scots Fusilier	6103
Punjab	5579	Royal Scots Grey	6101
Python	L5220	Royal Signals	5504
		Royal Sovereign	L5150
		Royal Tank Corps	5507
Q		Royal Ulster Rifleman	6122
Quail	L5369	Royal Welch Fusilier	6118
Quebec	5555	Rupert Guinness	L5915
Queen Alexandra	L5145		
Queen Elizabeth	6221	**S**	
Queen Empress	L5482	Saddleback	L5391
Queen Mary	6222	St. Dunstans	5501
Queen Mary	L5329	St. George	L5390
Queen Maud	6211	St. Helena	5624
Queen of the Belgians	L5648	St. Vincent	5686
Queensland	5566	Salopian	L5059
Queen's Westminster Rifleman	6162	Samson	5738
Queen Victoria's Rifleman	6160	Samson	6135

Samson	L5682	Sisyphus	L5520
Sandwich	5641	Skibo Castle	H14681
Sanspareil	5732	Skiddaw	L5098
Sanspareil	6126	Skiddaw Lodge	CW11568
Sanspareil	L5492	Smeaton	L5655
Saracen	L5507	Snaigow	H14522
Sarawak	5625	Snake	L5223
Sarmatian	L5454	Snipe	L5376
Saskatchewan	5561	Snowdon	L5001
Scorpion	L5295	Solomon Islands	5603
Scotia	L5704	Somaliland	5628
Scots Guardsman	6115	South Africa	5571
Scott	L5674	South Africa	L5355
Scottish Borderer	6104	South Australia	5567
Scottish Chief	L5473	Southern Rhodesia	5595
Seaforth Highlander	6108	Southport	5527
Seahorse	5705	Speke	L5029
Sedgwick	L5007	Sphinx	L5675
Senator	L5307	S. R. Graves	L5384
Servia	L5229	Staffordshire	L5542
Seychelles	5626	Staghound	L5353
Shakespeare	L5479	Stentor	L5723
Shamrock	L5302	Stephenson	5529
Shap	L5093	Stephenson	L5483
Shark	L5656	Stork	L5224
Sherwood Forester	6112	Straits Settlements	5629
Shooting Star	L5280	Strathcarron	H14274
Shovell	5651	Strathdearn	H14272
Shropshire	L5541	Strathpeffer	H15051
Sierra Leone	5627	Strathtay	H14273
Silver Jubilee	5552	Sturdee	5647
Simoom	L5308	Sultan	L5161
Sir Alexander Cockburn	L5062	Sunbeam	L5279
Sir Arthur Lawley	L5921	Superb	L5154
Sir Charles Cust	L6023	Suvla Bay	L5665
Sir Francis Dent	L5927	Swaziland	5630
Sir Frank Ree	5501	Swiftsure	5716
Sir Frank Ree	5530	Swiftsure	L5318
Sir Frank Ree	L5902	Sydney Smith	L5613
Sir Frederick Harrison	5524		
Sir Frederick Harrison	5531	**T**	
Sir Frederick Harrison	L5907	Talavera	L5018
Sir George	H14271	Talisman	L5975
Sir Gilbert Claughton	L5900	Tamerlane	L5285
Sir Guy Calthrop	L5923	Tanganyika	5631
Sir Hardman Earle	L5051	Tantalus	L5288
Sir Herbert Walker K.C.B.	5529	Tara	L5688
Sir Herbert Walker K.C.B.	5535	Tartarus	L5095
Sir Herbert Walker K.C.B.	L5926	Tasmania	5569
Sirius	L5107	Taymouth Castle	H14675
Sir James King	C14610	Telford	L5700
Sir James Thomson	C14751	Temeraire	L5158
Sir John French	L5646	Tennyson	L5943
Sirocco	L5297	Terrier	L5512
Sir Robert Turnbull	5540	Thalaba	L6002
Sir Robert Turnbull	L5901	The Artist's Rifleman	6164
Sir Thomas Brooke	L5325	The Auditor	L5042
Sir Thomas Williams	L5932	The Bedforshire and	
Sir William A. Stanier FRS	6256	Hertforshire Regiment	5516
Sir W. S. Gilbert	L5633	The Border Regiment	6136
Sister Dora	L5105	The Boy Scout	6169

The Cheshire Regiment	6134	Titan	L5276
The Duke of Wellington's Regt.		T. J. Hare	L5337
(West Riding)	6145	Tobago	5635
The Earl of Chester	L5094	Tonga	5632
The East Lancashire Regiment	6135	Tornado	L5481
The Girl Guide	6168	Trafalgar	5682
The Glasgow Highlander	5157	Trafalgar	L5170
The Green Howards	6133	Trans-Jordan	5633
The Hertforshire Regiment	6167	Travancore	5590
The Hussar	6154	Traveller	L5367
The Kings Dragoon Guardsman	6152	Trent	L5657
The King's Own	6161	Trentham	L5209
The King's Regiment Liverpool	6132	Trinidad	5634
The King's Royal Rifle Corps	6140	Tubal	L5244
The Lancer	6155	Typhon	L5396
The Leicestershire Regiment	5503	Tyrwhitt	5657
The Life Guardsman	6150		
The London Irish Rifleman	6138	**U**	
The Lovat Scouts	6128	Udiapur	5591
The Loyal Regiment	6158	Uganda	5636
The Manchester Regiment	6148	Ulster	5739
The Middlesex Regiment	6149	Unicorn	L5109
The Nile	L5653	United Provinces	5578
The Northamptonshire Regiment	6147	Urquhart Castle	H14686
The North Staffordshire Regiment	6141		
The Old Contemptible	6127	**V**	
Theorem	L5099	Valiant	5707
The Prince	2313	Vandal	L5194
The Prince of Wales's Volunteers		Vanguard	L5374
South Lancashire	6137	Velocipede	6148
The Princess Royal	6200	Velocipede	L5312
The Queen	L5032	Vernon	5661
The Ranger 12th London Regt.	6165	Vesta	6137
The Rifle Brigade	6146	Vesuvius	L5299
The Royal Air Force	6159	Victor	L5210
The Royal Army Ordnance Corps	5505	Victor Hugo	L5614
The Royal Artilleryman	6157	Victoria	5565
The Royal Dragoon	6153	Victoria	L5490
The Royal Horse Guardsman	6151	Victoria and Albert	L5118
The Royal Leicestershire Regiment	5503	Victorious	L5186
The Royal Pioneer Corps	5506	Victory	5712
The Royal Warwickshire Regiment	6131	Vimiera	L5024
The Scottish Horse	6129	Vindictive	5726
The South Staffordshire Regiment	6143	Vindictive	L5999
The South Wales Borderer	6156	Violet	L5092
The Welch Regiment	6139	Viscount	L5316
The West Yorkshire Regiment	6130	Vizier	L5221
The York & Lancaster Regiment	6142	Vulcan	6133
3rd Carabinier	6125	Vulcan	L5669
Thomas B. Macaulay	L5618	Vulture	L5215
Thomas Campbell	L5624		
Thomas Carlyle	L5045	**W**	
Thomas Gray	L5629	Warrior	L5147
Thomas Houghton	L5338	Warspite	5724
Thomas Moore	L5621	Warwickshire	L5543
Thomas Savery	L5517	Waterloo	L5080
Thunderbolt	L5193	Watt	L5236
Thunderer	5703	Waverley	L5203
Thunderer	L5310	W. C. Brocklehurst	L5326
Thurso Castle	H14688	W. E. Dorrington	L5911
Tiger	L5275		

Wellington	L5499	Witch	L5654
Welsh Guardsman	6117	W. M. Thackeray	L5630
Wemyss	5648	Wolfhound	L5341
Western Australia	5568	Wolverine	L5608
Westminster	L5330	Woodcock	L5379
Westmorland	L5544	Woodlark	L5104
Wheatstone	L5070	Worcestershire	L5549
Whitworth	L5081	Wordsworth	L5521
Widgeon	L5378	Wyre	L5108
Wild Duck	L5372		
Wildfire	L5086	**Y**	
William Cawkwell	L5484	Yorkshire	L5550
William Cowper	L5634		
William Froude	L5385	**Z**	
William Siemens	L5387	Zamiel	L5667
Windermere	L5401	Zanzibar	5638
Windward Islands	5637	Zillah	L5174